A CURIOUS COLLECTION OF WILD COMPANIONS

AN ILLUSTRATED ENCYCLOPEDIA

of INSEPARABLE SPECIES

SAMI BAYLY

THE EXPERIMENT

NEW YORK

CONTENTS

Introduction 4

African Death's-Head Hawkmoth
and Western Honey Bee 6

Ant Plant and Golden Ant 8

Australian Clownfish and
Bubble-Tip Anemone 10

Australian Garden Orb Weaver
Spider and Golden-Tipped Bat 12

Barnacle and Grey Whale 14

Blue-Banded Bee and
Climbing Guinea Flower 16

Boxer Crab and Sea Anemone 18

Brown-Throated Three-Toed
Sloth and Sloth Moth 20

Bullhorn Acacia and Acacia Ant 22

Canberra Grassland Earless Dragon
and Garden Wolf Spider 24

Candy Stripe Pistol Shrimp
and Black-Ray Goby 26

Cape Sugarbird and King Protea 28

Caribou and Arctic Fox 30

Cat, Brain Parasite, and Common Rat 32

Colombian Lesserblack Tarantula
and Dotted Humming Frog 34

Common Eastern Firefly and
Femme Fatale Firefly .36

Common Jack Mackerel and
Tongue-Biting Louse 38

Common Raven and Grey Wolf 40

Common Warthog and
Banded Mongoose 42

Drooping She-Oak and
Glossy Black Cockatoo 44

Eastern Screech-Owl and
Texas Blind Snake 46

Egyptian Spiny-Tailed Lizard
and Arabian Fattail Scorpion 48

Emperor Shrimp and Spanish Dancer 50

Emu and Desert Quandong 52

Eucalyptus Tree, Bell Miner, and Psyllid 54

Fire Urchin and Carrier Crab 56

Floreana Lava Lizard and Marine Iguana...58

Flowering Eucalyptus and
Little Red Flying Fox.....................60

Galapagos Dove and Opuntia Cactus........62

Golden Jackal and Bengal Tiger 64

Grass Trigger Plant and Reed Bee........66

Grazing Animals and Cattle Egret..........68

Green-Banded Broodsac and Amber Snail...70

Green Sea Turtle and Yellow Tang.........72

Heath's Tick and
Mountain Pygmy Possum..................74

Kinkajou and Balsa Tree..................76

Laysan Albatross and Ocean Sunfish.......78

Leadbeater's Possum and Goblin Flea.......80

Leopard Coral Grouper and
Bluestreak Cleaner Wrasse.................82

Leopard Sea Cucumber
and Pinhead Pearlfish.....................84

Monarch Butterfly and Viceroy Butterfly....86

Moreton Bay Fig and Fig Wasp...........88

Northern Bettong and Truffles............90

Oak Tree and Eastern Chipmunk..........92

Oceanic Whitetip Shark and Pilot Fish......94

Painted Honeyeater and Grey Mistletoe....96

Pea Crab and Blue Mussel.................98

Pink-Tailed Worm-Lizard
and Tyrant Ant...........................100

Pitcher Plant and Mountain Treeshrew.....102

Pseudoscorpion and Giant Harlequin Beetle.104

Red Weaver Ant and Soft Scale Bug......106

Sea Squirt and Spotted Handfish.........108

Sponge Decorator Crab and Sea Sponge...110

Stinking Corpse Lily and Liana Vine.......112

Sweet Bursaria, Eltham Copper Butterfly,
and Notoncus Ant.......................114

Tea Tree and Lord Howe
Island Stick Insect.........................116

Vampire Finch and Nazca Booby..........118

Verco's Nudibranch and Bryozoan........120

White Suckerfish and Reef Manta Ray....122

Yucca Plant and Yucca Moth.............124

Resources.................................126

About the Author 127

INTRODUCTION

*I*nside this illustrated encyclopedia you'll uncover some of the most bizarre, wonderful, and downright disturbing creature connections nature has to offer. Companionship in the wild—known as "symbiois"—comes in many forms. The simplest, happiest kind of friendship is called "mutualism," which is when different animals or plants share a relationship that mutually benefits them both throughout their lives. But that's only the beginning; relationships can be complicated, and it's no different in the natural world! Pairings among plants and animals fall into three categories.

MUTUALISM: Both sides of the partnership benefit from their relationship.

COMMENSALISM: Only one side of the partnership benefits from their relationship, while the other is unaffected.

PARASITISM: One side of the partnership benefits and the other is negatively affected.

Within these categories there are further distinctions.

OBLIGATE MUTUALISM: The pair cannot survive without one another.

FACULTATIVE MUTUALISM: Both sides of the partnership can survive on their own, but it is more beneficial for the pair to stay together.

MÜLLERIAN MIMICRY: Two or more unrelated toxic, or poisonous, creatures evolve to resemble one another.

INQUILINISM (COMMENSALISM): One side of the partnership permanently lives on the other.

PHORESY (COMMENSALISM): One side of the partnership uses the other as a means of transportation.

PREDATION: One side of the partnership preys upon and kills the other side, usually as a key food source in its diet.

You will find examples of all these curious behaviors in this book. As with my previous books in this series, *A Curious Collection of Peculiar Creatures* and *A Curious Collection of Dangerous Creatures*, I hope you'll see the natural world as I do, filled with astonishing, inspiring, and downright weird (in a good way!) plants and animals. With so many of their habitats endangered around the world, they're counting on us to discover all the amazing ways they've adapted to work together to survive—so that we can help them, too!

Sami Bayly

AFRICAN DEATH'S-HEAD HAWKMOTH

WESTERN HONEY BEE

COMMENSALISM

Acherontia atropos
(a-ker-on-tee-a a-tro-pos)

Apis mellifera
(a-piss mel-if-er-a)

With a wingspan of 3.5 to 5 inches (9–13 cm), the African death's-head hawkmoth is much larger than the western honey bee, whose wingspan measures less than an inch (1–2 cm) across. But that doesn't stop the hawkmoth from pretending to be a bee so it can steal the precious honey from their hives! How does it trick the bees? First, it camouflages itself with a chemical scent that makes it smell just like a honey bee. Second, it makes a high-pitched squeak, or chirp, that may mimic a sound the queen bee makes to calm the worker bees. If the hawkmoth is discovered, though, the bees will turn against the intruder and kill it.

Conservation Status

UNKNOWN/ DATA DEFICIENT

Researchers have not determined the conservation status of the African death's-head hawkmoth or the western honey bee. However, we do know that insecticides used to kill pests often end up killing hawkmoths instead. Parasites also target them in their larval stage, before they turn into moths. Honey bees can be poisoned by chemicals or harmed by mite infestations.

What They Eat

Hawkmoths eat honey from the beehives they sneak into and nectar from tobacco and potato flowers. Western honey bee larvae that are fed nectar and pollen will develop into worker bees, while the larvae that are fed nectar, pollen, and royal jelly (a white, jellylike substance secreted by worker bees) will turn into queens.

Where They Live

This pair is found in parts of Africa and the Middle East, including Egypt and Israel, and also in areas of Europe like France and Spain. The hawkmoth inhabits dry, open fields, while honey bees like to nest in tree hollows. Many subspecies of western honey bee can be found across the globe.

FUN FACTS

✦ The hawkmoth can fly up to 30 miles (48 km) per hour—faster than any other moth in the world!

✦ Thanks to their sinister appearance—they have a pattern on their thorax that looks like a skull—the hawkmoth has long been considered an omen of death or misfortune.

✦ The collective noun for a group of moths is a "whisper."

✦ The hawkmoth uses its proboscis, a long mouthpart that's shaped like a tube, to drink honey and nectar.

ANT PLANT

GOLDEN ANT

MUTUALISM

Myrmecodia beccarii
(mer-me-co-dee-a beck-ar-ee-eye)

Philidris cordata
(fill-ee-driss core-dat-a)

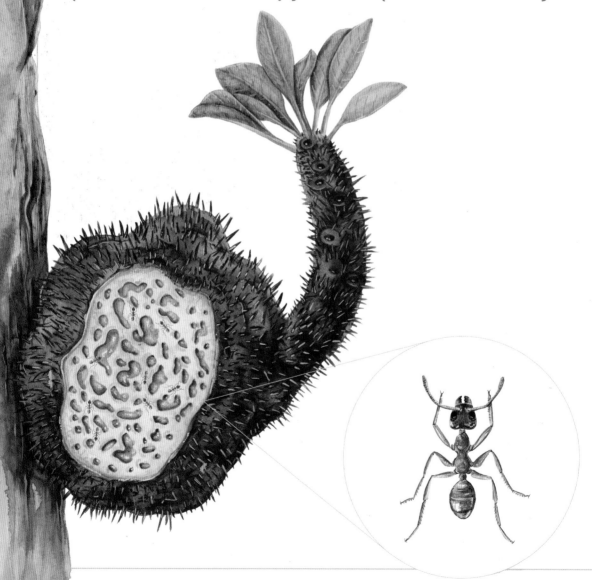

The tiny golden ant, less than half an inch long (9 mm), needs a well-protected home, and the ant plant needs a suitable tenant to help feed it. The ant plant is an "epiphyte," or air plant, a curious type of plant that doesn't grow out of the ground but lives on another plant without harming it. It is pictured here growing on a tree. The illustration shows a cross section of the ant plant with its numerous intricate tunnels and chambers—ideal living quarters for the golden ant. The ants leave their droppings in these cool, dark spaces, as well as any leftover food, both of which provide extra nutrients that are absorbed by the plant. These help the ant plant flourish in its forest home.

Conservation Status

VULNERABLE / UNKNOWN

Golden ants are plentiful, but the ant plant is threatened by invasive weeds and habitat loss. Action must be taken to avoid losing even more of these incredible plants.

What They Eat

The flowers and fruit of the ant plant attract not only golden ants, but other insects, too—and these make a tasty meal for the ants. The ant plant gets its food supply and nutrients from the ants' dung and food scraps. It's a truly symbiotic relationship!

Where They Live

Found only in Australia, the ant plant is native to northern Cape York and the Cairns region, where it grows on the soft trunks of casuarinas and melaleucas in mangrove or lowland forest habitats. The golden ant can be found in Australia, Papua New Guinea, and other Pacific Islands, but only in Australia does it call the ant plant home.

FUN FACTS

◆ There is another creature that depends on the ant plant and the golden ant for its survival. The Apollo jewel butterfly lays its eggs on the ant plant. The eggs have the same scent as ant larvae, so the ants are tricked into caring for the eggs.

◆ The fruit of the ant plant is eaten by the mistletoebird. After digesting the seeds, the bird poops them out in another location, generally high up in a tree. This is how ant plants spread.

AUSTRALIAN CLOWNFISH

BUBBLE-TIP ANEMONE

MUTUALISM

Amphiprion rubrocinctus
(am-fip-ree-on rub-ro-sink-tus)

Entacmaea quadricolor
(en-tack-me-a quad-ree-color)

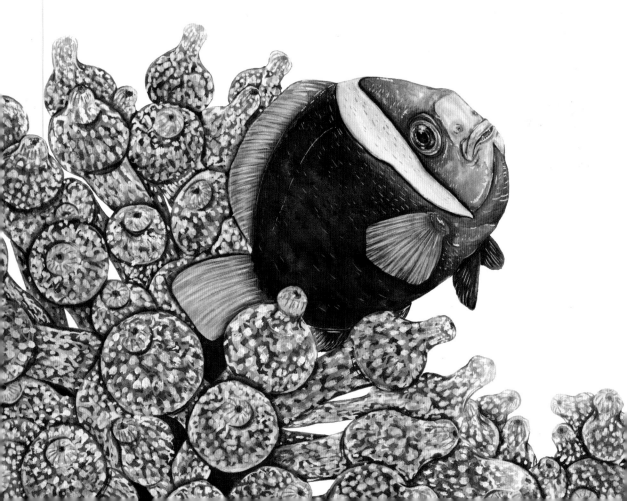

The bubble-tip anemone may look charmingly colorful—and it has such a harmless-sounding name—but if you spot one in the waters off the coast of Australia, beware! Touching it will give you quite a sting. Unless you're an Australian clownfish, that is. This little orange fish makes its home inside the anemone's swaying tentacles, where it's kept safe from predators. It's able to do this thanks to a layer of protective mucus that makes it immune to the anemone's poison. The anemone benefits, too. The clownfish helps it out by munching on parasites and chasing off fish that try to snack on its tentacles. Plus, the clownfish fertilizes the anemone with its nitrogen-rich poop, and even helps it get enough oxygen at night by fanning its fins!

Conservation Status

LEAST CONCERN/ UNKNOWN

Both the Australian clownfish and the bubble-tip anemone have a stable population, but there are looming threats to their habitats, such as coral bleaching. Bleaching happens when a change in environment causes coral to become stressed, and it eventually destroys the coral reef. It is vital to protect these habitats for all the animals that live in them.

What They Eat

Australian clownfish enjoy plucking food or parasites out of the water around them. The rest of their diet is made up mainly of algae, passing debris, plankton, and small invertebrates. The anemone survives on nutrients created by algae that lives in its body, called zooxanthellae (pronounced "zo-ah-zan-thel-ee").

Where They Live

Native to the northwestern regions of Australia, including the western Gulf of Carpentaria and the North West Cape, the Australian clownfish hides at depths of 3 to 26 feet (1–8 m). You might spot it tucked within the bubble-tip anemone in lagoons and coastal reefs. The anemone usually buries its base in a crevice so that only its tentacles are visible, making it safer from potential predators.

FUN FACTS

◆ Clownfish are also called "anemonefish" because of their close relationship with anemones.

◆ Male clownfish guard the eggs of their offspring, using their tails to fan oxygen toward them until they are ready to hatch.

◆ The symbiotic relationship between the clownfish and the anemone was made famous by the movie *Finding Nemo!*

AUSTRALIAN GARDEN ORB WEAVER SPIDER

GOLDEN-TIPPED BAT

PARASITISM

Eriophora transmarina
(er-ee-o-for-a trans-mar-ee-na)

Phoniscus papuensis
(fon-is-cus pap-oo-en-sis)

*T*he golden-tipped bat feeds almost exclusively on spiders that it catches in the dead of night—and the meal it loves most is the Australian garden orb weaver, a 2-inch-long (5 cm) spider that builds a large round web. To keep from getting caught in these strong, sticky webs, the bat has small, round-tipped wings and a tail membrane that together allow it to hover in the air, fly slowly, and make tight turns. It finds the spiders by making high-pitched sounds and then using the sound waves that bounce back to guide it—a system called "echolocation." Once it's homed in on its eight-legged prey, the bat snatches the spider from its web, dodging the dangerous threads in a cunning feat of predation (see page 5). The garden orb weaver makes up 95 percent of the bat's diet—without these spiders, it could not survive.

Conservation Status

UNKNOWN/VARIED

The golden-tipped bat has become endangered because its habitat is being destroyed; it's also hunted by feral and pet cats. An increase in the frequency of bushfires has impacted both the golden-tipped bat and the Australian garden orb weaver, which is listed as vulnerable in New South Wales.

What They Eat

Aside from Australian garden orb weavers, the golden-tipped bat will also eat long-jawed spiders and the occasional moth, insect, or butterfly. The bats seem to use their needle-sharp teeth to pierce the spiders' bodies and suck out the insides. The diet of the Australian garden orb weaver consists of flying insects that it captures in its web.

Where They Live

The golden-tipped bat is found in Australia and Papua New Guinea. In Australia, it is most abundant in the east, where it roosts in trees and hollows in rain forests or other wet, woody habitats. Australian garden orb weavers construct their webs between trees or shrubs every evening and take them down at dawn.

FUN FACTS

◆ Golden-tipped bats will fly as far as a mile (2 km) from their nests to find food.

◆ Rather than building their own nests, these bats hijack empty bird nests.

◆ The Australian garden orb weaver has a life span of only one year.

◆ Due to their fantastic dodging skills, golden-tipped bats are able to avoid most of the trapping gear set out by researchers hoping to learn more about them, so there is still a lot to learn about this elusive species.

BARNACLE GREY WHALE

COMMENSALISM

Cryptolepas rhachianecti
(crip-toll-ee-pas rach-ian-ect-ee)

Eschrichtius robustus
(es-cry-chee-us row-bus-tus)

*T*he whale barnacle, which measures no more than three quarters of an inch (1–2.5 cm) across, is picky when it comes to its host. It attaches itself almost exclusively to the grey whale, a massive mammal that can reach 39 feet (12 m) long and can weigh more than 44 tons (40,000 kg). The whale is an ideal home for the barnacle, which gets to hitch a free ride through the ocean, catching food that floats by without expending any energy. And the barnacle doesn't harm the whale in the slightest. Since the barnacle uses the whale as a form of transportation, this relationship is an example of "phoresy" (see page 5).

Conservation Status

UNKNOWN/ LEAST CONCERN

Although listed as least concern, the grey whale is thought to be extinct in many parts of the world. They have disappeared from the oceans around the United Kingdom, Korea, and Iceland as a result of commercial whaling or being accidentally caught in fishing gear. They are also sometimes eaten by killer whales.

What They Eat

Barnacles may be small, but they have a big appetite! To eat, they poke out their feathery feet and catch any plankton floating past. The grey whale eats lots of tiny, wiggling oceanic life-forms you may not have heard of before, including tube-dwelling amphipods, swarming mysids, and polychaete tube worms. The whales have also been known to eat fish eggs, baitfish, and crabs.

Where They Live

Barnacles will crowd the vast body of a grey whale over its lifetime, gravitating to the whale's tail, back, flippers, and head. Grey whales live in waters around the world, including those near Canada, the United States, Mexico, Russia, China, and Japan. Your best chance to see one is along the coast, as they usually don't swim too far out to sea.

FUN FACTS

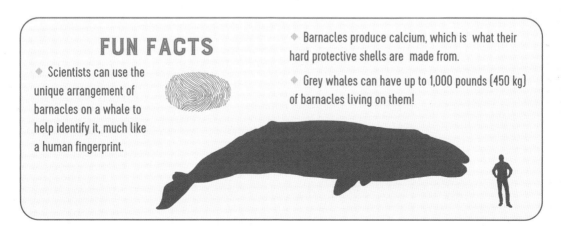

⬥ Scientists can use the unique arrangement of barnacles on a whale to help identify it, much like a human fingerprint.

⬥ Barnacles produce calcium, which is what their hard protective shells are made from.

⬥ Grey whales can have up to 1,000 pounds (450 kg) of barnacles living on them!

BLUE-BANDED BEE

CLIMBING GUINEA FLOWER

MUTUALISM

Amegilla cingulata
(am-eg-ill-a sing-you-lat-a)

Hibbertia scandens
(hib-ber-sha scan-dens)

*T*he relationship between the blue-banded bee and the climbing guinea flower—a vine that features bright yellow blooms of 2 to 3 inches (5–7 cm) across—is a special one. The little fuzzy bee, which sports striking stripes of blue and black on its abdomen, uses a pollination technique called "buzz pollination." When the bee lands on a flower, it attaches itself firmly to the blossom with its legs; then it moves its wing muscles very quickly, creating a vibration that shakes the flower's pollen loose. The climbing guinea flower is unable to release its pollen any other way, so without the blue-banded bee, it wouldn't be able to reproduce!

Conservation Status

UNKNOWN/UNKNOWN

Blue-banded bees have natural predators such as birds, spiders, dragonflies, and assassin bugs. Like many bee species worldwide, their numbers are also threatened by climate change, pollution, and pesticides. It is very important that we ensure the survival of bees, as they play a crucial role in the ecosystem.

What They Eat

The blue-banded bee sips nectar from flowers; it mixes the nectar with pollen to feed its young. While the climbing guinea flower is its favorite plant, the bee will also visit sennas and nightshades, as well as the mountain devil, the yellow flame tree, lavender, rosemary, kiwifruit, and blueberry.

Where They Live

This pair is native to Australia. The flower grows from southeast New South Wales up to northeast Queensland, while the bee is found across all of Australia except Tasmania. The climbing guinea flower enjoys a mixture of sandy coastal habitats and sheltered forest environments. Blue-banded bees prefer to nest in soft sandstone cliffs. In human-populated areas, they will also build their nests in clay or mud-brick homes.

FUN FACTS

◆ Female blue-banded bees are solitary creatures, nesting alone. The male bees live in small groups.

◆ Count the stripes to tell the difference between male and female blue-banded bees! Male bees have five blue bands, and females have four.

◆ The climbing guinea flower gets its common name from its resemblance to the guinea, a vibrant gold coin first made in Great Britain in 1663.

◆ Stop and smell the . . . mothballs? Some people find the climbing guinea flower's odor sweet, others detect a hint of something foul—even urine or cow dung!

BOXER CRAB

SEA ANEMONE

MUTUALISM

Lybia tessellata
(lie-bee-a tess-ell-a-ta)

Triactis producta
(try-act-us pro-duck-ta)

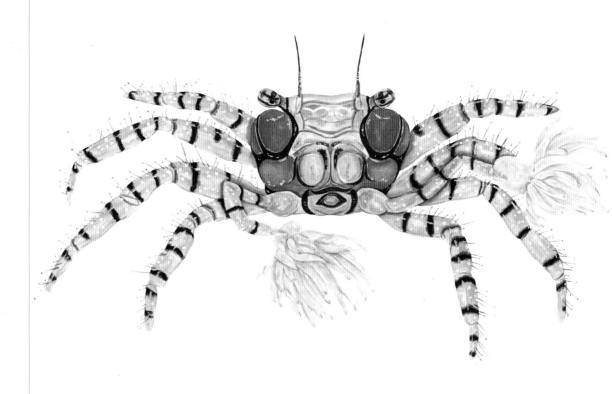

*A*lso known as the pom-pom crab, this cute crustacean is truly tiny—it measures just under an inch (2.5 cm) across—but it packs a punch thanks to two even smaller stinging anemones that it grips in its claws. By thrusting the poisonous anemones at predators, the crab can defend itself. But the anemones play another role as well. The crab's claws have evolved for only one purpose—to hold the anemones—and they are too small and frail to grab the particles of food that float by. So the crab uses the anemones' tentacles to snag its snacks. The sea anemone may also benefit from this partnership: It gains more oxygen from being waved about, and the crab moves it to new locations where it can find more food.

Conservation Status

UNKNOWN/UNKNOWN

The conservation status of both the boxer crab and the sea anemone is unknown, so they are probably not in any immediate danger of extinction. We can safely assume the pair face threats from climate change and habitat destruction, as well as the risk of being eaten by larger fish, sharks, octopuses, and more.

What They Eat

The boxer crab is an omnivore, eating plant and other organic matter drifting through the ocean, which it collects in the sea anemone's tendrils. Any food that the crab doesn't eat goes to the anemone.

Where They Live

These creatures are found in the tropical Indo-Pacific Ocean, including areas around the Red Sea, the East African coastline, Indonesia, Australia, and New Guinea. The boxer crab and the sea anemone inhabit shallow waters with sandy seabeds and use their well-camouflaged bodies to blend in. When the sea anemone is not in the grasp of the crab, it suctions itself onto rocks and dead coral.

FUN FACTS

◆ This sea anemone is extremely poisonous, so it's no surprise that it successfully wards off predators. A sting from its tentacles can cause severe pain, swelling, and even blisters.

◆ If the crab loses one of its anemones, it will split the remaining anemone in half. In just a few days, both pieces will regenerate into whole anemones.

◆ The boxer crab has become dependent on the sea anemone to function. Without it, the crab cannot fight or feed, as their claws are too weak.

BROWN-THROATED THREE-TOED SLOTH

SLOTH MOTH

MUTUALISM

Bradypus variegatus
(brad-ee-pus var-ee-gate-us)

Cryptoses choloepi
(crip-toe-sees kol-ee-pie)

*T*he long, coarse hair of the three-toed sloth is more than just fur—it's home to a complex ecosystem of living creatures, including a small flying insect called the sloth moth and a kind of green algae! As its name suggests, the sloth moth only lives on sloths, and the more moths there are in a sloth's fur, the more algae there is. This is good for the sloth, as the algae helps to camouflage it and also serves as a source of extra nutrition. When this slow-moving mammal makes its weekly trip down from the treetops to use the toilet, the female moths lay their eggs on the sloth's fresh dung. Eventually, baby moths will hatch and fly up into the tree canopy, looking for their own sloth to live on.

Conservation Status

LEAST CONCERN/ UNKNOWN

The brown-throated three-toed sloth occupies large areas of many protected habitats, so it is not currently listed as endangered. However, its habitat in Colombia and the Atlantic Forest, along the east coast of South America, are both facing deforestation. Sadly, this has already impacted the sloth's population. They also face threats from harpy eagles, cars, and poachers.

What They Eat

Sloths move very, very slowly. This is due to their herbivorous diet of leaves, flowers, and fruits. They don't need to drink—the water they absorb from plant matter provides all the hydration they need.

Where They Live

Brown-throated three-toed sloths are native to southern Central America and South America, including Bolivia, Brazil, Colombia, Ecuador, and Honduras. They can be found in a variety of forest environments, including lowland tropical, semi-deciduous, and low-level cloud forests.

FUN FACTS

◆ Sloths sleep for up to 15 hours a day. And it can take an entire month for a sloth to digest a single meal!

◆ Sloths can turn their necks up to 270 degrees, while humans can turn theirs only 180 degrees.

◆ Sloths' peg-shaped teeth continue growing throughout their lives.

◆ Although they can barely walk on land, sloths are surprisingly strong swimmers!

BULLHORN ACACIA

ACACIA ANT

MUTUALISM

Vachellia cornigera
(va-chel-ee-a corn-ee-ger-a)

Pseudomyrmex ferruginea
(soo-do-merr-mex fer-oo-gin-ee-a)

*T*he bullhorn acacia is a towering tree that grows to around 30 feet (10 m) tall. It gets its name from the spiky, deep-red thorns on its branches that resemble a bull's horns and look like they could hurt you. The acacia ant is smaller than a grain of rice, only about 3 millimeters long, and it seems too tiny to hurt anything. But it's the acacia ant that protects the bullhorn acacia! Up to 16,000 ants live on each tree, keeping it safe from other insects, plants, and pests that could harm it. In exchange, the bullhorn acacia provides the ants with nectar and nutrients and lets them live safely inside its sharp, hollow thorns. Neither one could survive without the other—an example of an obligate mutualistic relationship (see page 4).

Conservation Status

UNKNOWN/UNKNOWN

Acacia ants are fiercely territorial, so they'll scare away any creature that has plans to eat the bullhorn acacia—whether a hungry cow, horse, or caterpillar. This significantly lessens the dangers the tree faces, but the acacia is still vulnerable to human-related threats, such as habitat destruction.

What They Eat

Acacia ants feed on the sweet, sticky nectar at the base of the acacia's leaves, and on proteins and fatty acids that are produced by the plant. Eating this food doesn't hurt the tree, making it the perfect payback for the security service the ants provide.

Where They Live

The habitat of the acacia ant and the bullhorn acacia ranges from southern Mexico all the way down to Costa Rica. They live and grow in swamplands, pastures, and even along roadsides. Many bullhorn acacias start from seeds dispersed throughout the countryside in bird poop.

FUN FACTS

◆ If you are bitten by an acacia ant, you will know it. Their bites can cause a painful stinging sensation, as well as swelling, throbbing, and prolonged itchiness.

◆ It can be dangerous for animals to eat the leaves of many acacia species, because in times of drought they store high amounts of cyanide, a toxic chemical.

◆ Humans can eat the tasty pulp surrounding the acacia's seedpods.

◆ The bark of many acacia species is also used for medicinal purposes: to treat wounds, as mouthwash, and even to stop diarrhea.

3 millimeters

23

CANBERRA GRASSLAND EARLESS DRAGON

GARDEN WOLF SPIDER

COMMENSALISM

Tympanocryptis lineata
(tim-pan-o-crip-tus lin-ee-ay-ta)

Tasmanicosa godeffroyi
(tas-man-eeco-sa go-def-roy-eye)

*T*he Canberra grassland earless dragon is a small, spiny lizard whose favorite place to live is in the abandoned burrow of the garden wolf spider. After building its burrow, the spider spends most of its short life hiding in it before eventually moving out. That's when the earless dragon moves in. The lizard uses the spider's burrow as a place to sleep, hide from predators, reset its body temperature, mate, and eat. But sometimes the dragon gets a little ahead of itself, venturing into burrows that have not yet been vacated and becoming the wolf spider's new housemate, resulting in what must be a tight squeeze.

Conservation Status

LEAST CONCERN/ UNKNOWN

From the time of European settlement, Australian native grasslands have been severely compromised by agriculture, invasive predators, weeds, drought, and bushfires. These threats have had a dramatic impact on the Canberra grassland earless dragon, and if we are not careful, they will impact garden wolf spiders, too.

What They Eat

The garden wolf spider has a diet made up of ants, crickets, beetles, and moths. The Canberra grassland earless dragon has a similar diet: It eats small insects and spiders.

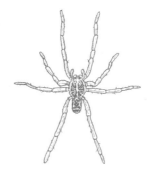

Where They Live

The grassland earless dragon lives in native grassland plains in a region near Australia's capital city of Canberra. If you are lucky enough to spot one, it will most likely be residing in a spider's burrow or hiding under a rock. Many of these grasslands have been turned into farms or housing, destroying these animals' habitats. Fortunately, garden wolf spiders are abundant and can be found across most coastal areas of Australia.

FUN FACTS

◆ The garden wolf spider is often called the Union Jack spider thanks to the black-and-white pattern on its back, which resembles the design on the British flag.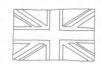

◆ The collective noun for a group of spiders is a "cluster."

◆ The garden wolf spider produces enough venom to cause painful and deadly bites to animals, and severe pain, dizziness, and swelling in humans as well.

◆ The Canberra grassland earless dragon was rediscovered in 1991 after not being seen for 30 years.

CANDY STRIPE PISTOL SHRIMP

BLACK-RAY GOBY

MUTUALISM

Alpheus randalli
(al-fee-us ran-dal-ee)

Stonogobiops nematodes
(ston-o-go-bi-ops nem-a-toads)

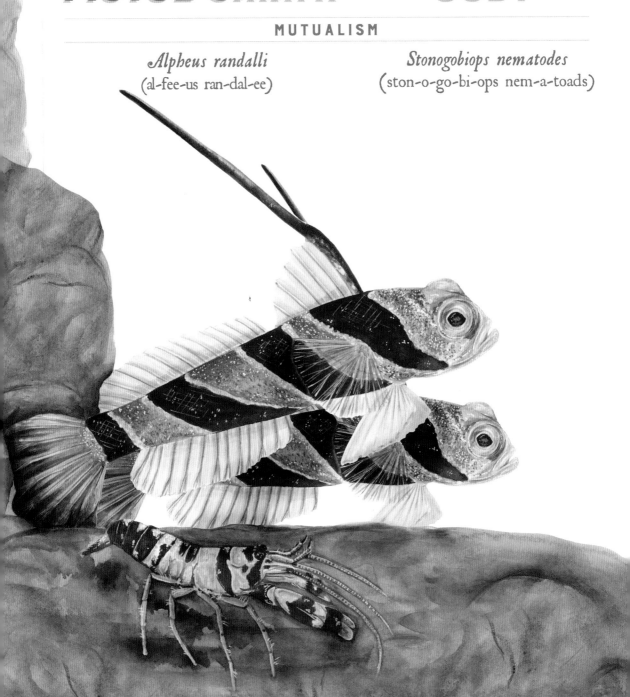

The candy stripe pistol shrimp is far from defenseless—it has an extra-large left claw that it can snap shut, producing a powerful jet of water and a sound that's louder than a gunshot. Together, these effects stun prey and scare off predators. But the shrimp has one significant weakness: It's nearly blind. That's where the black-ray goby comes in. This little fish serves as the "eyes" for the shrimp, standing guard at the opening to its burrow and watching for predators. As the busy shrimp takes care of its home, it uses its antennae to keep in constant contact with the goby. When a predator approaches, the goby twitches its tail, telling the shrimp to hide, and then darts into the shelter itself. In return for the goby's work as a bodyguard, the shrimp lets the fish live in its burrow.

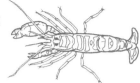

Conservation Status

UNKNOWN/LEAST CONCERN

Fortunately, neither the candy stripe pistol shrimp nor the black-ray goby face many threats. However, they are impacted by habitat destruction, changing water temperatures, and the aquarium trade, which the goby is often sold into.

What They Eat

The candy stripe pistol shrimp likes to eat small parasites, scraps, and sometimes even smaller shrimp. The black-ray goby feeds on small creatures like zooplankton and invertebrates that it finds on the sandy ocean floor.

Where They Live

Native to the Indo-Pacific and western Indian Ocean, the black-ray goby and the candy stripe pistol shrimp can be found off the coast of Indonesia, Thailand, Malaysia, China, and Japan. The pair prefer to reside from 36 to 180 feet (11–55 m) deep, in sandy, rubble-strewn caves.

FUN FACTS

◆ Black-ray gobys live in mated pairs, so it is common to see two living in a burrow with the pistol shrimp.

◆ The black-ray goby is often kept in aquariums and has been known to jump out of tanks without lids.

◆ The pistol shrimp can snap its left claw shut at a speed of 60 miles (97 km) per hour, creating a pulse of water that can reach 8,672°F (4,800°C), nearly as hot as the surface of the sun!

CAPE SUGARBIRD

KING PROTEA

MUTUALISM

Promerops cafer
(pro-mer-ops ca-fer)

Protea cynaroides
(pro-tee-a sin-a-roy-dees)

The king protea has evolved over many years in tandem with the Cape sugarbird, a nectar-eating bird that serves as the plant's main pollinator. This sugarbird nests among the protea leaves, waiting for the flowers to bloom. Once they do, the bird sips the blossoms' nectar using its long beak; as it drinks the sweet syrup, its feathers are dusted with pollen. After it has finished feeding on one flower, it moves to the next, pollinating the plant in the process. This is an example of facultative mutualism (see page 5): The pair could survive without each other, but both benefit from their partnership.

Conservation Status

LEAST CONCERN/ LEAST CONCERN

The Cape sugarbird has a stable population, and the king protea is listed as least concern. However, this is not necessarily the case for many other species in the Proteaceae family. Around half of the protea species in Africa are believed to be endangered, either because their habitats are being destroyed or because they are being overpicked for their decorative flowers.

What They Eat

The Cape sugarbird eats nectar, and the bird will feed insects to its young, such as the green protea beetle. Protea plants have evolved a useful technique to stay hydrated in the harsh, dry environment they grow in—they absorb water from coastal fog that passes by.

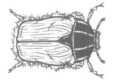

Where They Live

Proteas are native to South Africa, where the king protea grows in rocky, acidic soil in the Eastern Cape and Western Cape provinces. The Cape sugarbird and the king protea thrive in the Cape Floristic Region, a protected area mainly made up of shrubland habitat that's prone to fire. Protea flowers are also cultivated in many other countries due to their beautiful appearance.

FUN FACTS

◆ The king protea is South Africa's national flower.

◆ The blossoms of the king protea are gigantic— they measure from 6 to 12 inches (15–30 cm) across!

◆ The Proteaceae family is one of the oldest families of flowering plants. Scientists believe proteas have been around for 300 million years.

◆ The male Cape sugarbird has a remarkably long tail that can measure up to 15 inches (38 cm) long!

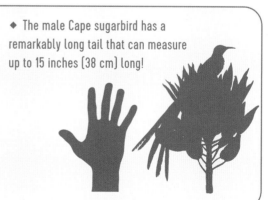

CARIBOU   ARCTIC FOX

COMMENSALISM

Rangifer tarandus
(ran-gi-fer tar-ran-dus)

Vulpes lagopus
(vul-pes lag-o-pus)

The caribou and the Arctic fox live in very cold climates, and during the winter, it can be difficult to find food. But the clever fox has a trick up its furry white sleeve! It follows the caribou through the snow and waits as the large deer digs up the frozen ground with its hooves, in search of the plants that make up its winter diet. As it digs, it also unearths tiny rodents like mice and shrews, which live in burrows under the snow to stay warm and safe from predators—like the Arctic fox! The fox moves in, pounces on its prey, and takes home dinner.

Conservation Status

VULNERABLE/ LEAST CONCERN

Caribou spend much of their lives traveling across huge distances. So, when humans build houses, highways, fences, and other structures in the caribou's habitat, the deer can't go where they need to go. This is one of the reasons their numbers have dropped over the years. Habitat destruction, climate change, and fur hunting all threaten the Arctic fox, but its population is currently at a healthy size.

What They Eat

Arctic foxes are opportunistic feeders, which means they will eat almost anything they can find! Rodents, ptarmigans, lemmings, eggs, berries, insects, and leftover animal remains, or "carrion," are all on the menu. Caribou eat only lichen and fungi in the winter. During the warmer months, these herbivores eat grass, moss, ferns, shrubs, and tree leaves.

Where They Live

Caribou live in North America and in Europe, where they are called reindeer. Arctic foxes live in the Arctic tundra, a treeless ecosystem found only in the northern regions of Alaska, Canada, Russia, Greenland, Iceland, and Scandinavia. They build burrows called "dens" that are shared by many generations of foxes.

FUN FACTS

◆ The collective noun for a group of caribou is a "herd." The collective noun for a group of Arctic foxes is a "skulk" or a "leash."

◆ A caribou will travel 2,000 miles (3,220 km), on average, in just one year!

◆ The Arctic fox uses its long, fluffy tail as a blanket, wrapping it around its body to keep itself warm.

◆ In most species of deer, only the male grows antlers. But female caribou have antlers, too!

CAT   BRAIN PARASITE   COMMON RAT

PARASITISM

Felis catus
(feel-us cat-us)

Toxoplasma gondii
(tox-o-plas-ma gon-dee-eye)

Rattus norvegicus
(rat-us nor-veg-ee-cus)

The cat, the common rat, and a tiny parasite called *Toxoplasma gondii* are all connected in a complex cycle. It starts when a rat consumes cat poop or urine infected with the microscopic parasite. Once inside the rat, the single-celled organism reworks the fear receptors in the rodent's brain, telling it that cats aren't dangerous—and even tricking it into thinking of felines as potential mates! Obviously, it won't take long for a cat to catch and eat a rat that's been taken over by the mind-controlling parasite. And that's exactly what the parasite needs. Once it's found its way into another cat, it can reproduce and continue its life cycle. After a few days, the parasite's eggs, or "cysts," will be shed in the cat's poop or urine for another rat to eat.

Conservation Status

UNKNOWN/UNKNOWN/ LEAST CONCERN

The cat, the rat, and *Toxoplasma gondii* can be found all over the world, and their populations are not considered to be under any threat. The common rat, which once inhabited only northern China, has now spread to every continent except Antarctica!

What They Eat

This parasite survives off proteins found in its host's cells. A rat's usual diet consists of seeds, fruits, and plants, but in urban areas they are known to eat pet food, human food, and even garbage. Domestic cats typically eat cat food, but often hunt birds and small mammals such as mice and rats.

Where They Live

The cat tends to live with or near humans, and is one of our most beloved pets. The common rat also likes to live near people, often in sewers or subways under our cities. The mind-controlling parasite can live in all kinds of animals, including cattle, sea otters, and even humans! You can avoid getting this parasite by not touching cat poop or pee and by washing your hands after cleaning a cat's litter box.

FUN FACTS

◆ At least 40 million people in the United States are believed to carry this parasite. It doesn't harm people with strong immune systems, but pregnant women and other people with lowered immunity should be careful not to contract it.

◆ The parasite causes permanent changes to rodents' brains—even after the parasite can't be detected in its body, a previously infected rat will display no fear of cats.

COLOMBIAN LESSERBLACK TARANTULA

DOTTED HUMMING FROG

COMMENSALISM

Xenesthis immanis
(zen-es-this im-man-is)

Chiasmocleis ventrimaculata
(ky-as-mo-kle-us ven-tri-mak-you-la-ta)

This pair's relationship is truly remarkable, as a spider as large as the hairy Colombian lesserblack tarantula would usually make a quick meal out of a little frog, not make friends with it! But the dotted humming frog actually shares a burrow with this purple-and-black spider. There, the tiny trilling amphibian dines on leftovers from the spider's meals and receives protection from predators like snakes. Why doesn't the tarantula eat the frog? Scientists believe it may be because the frog keeps the spider's eggs safe from ants. Or it may be because the frog's skin secretes a toxin that makes it a less-than-tasty treat. No one knows for sure—so while this may be a mutualistic relationship in which both parties benefit, it's still technically considered commensalism.

Conservation Status

UNKNOWN/ LEAST CONCERN

Although these two animals are not listed as endangered, their populations can vary greatly depending on where you look. Unfortunately, their habitats are being logged and destroyed faster and faster in order to use the land for agriculture.

What They Eat

Hiding at the entrance of its burrow at night, the Colombian lesserblack tarantula will ambush any prey unfortunate enough to pass by. This can include insects, geckos, and even other spiders. The dotted humming frog eats ants, insects, and any of the spider's leftovers.

Where They Live

The dotted humming frog and the Colombian lesserblack tarantula are found in northern and central Bolivia, Peru, Colombia, and parts of Brazil. They like to live in leaf litter near swamps and ponds in tropical rain forests. Both the tarantula and the frog are burrowing species and will spend most of the day hidden away, only surfacing in the safety of darkness.

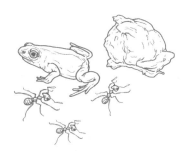

FUN FACTS

◆ Male Colombian lesserblack tarantulas live for 3.5 years, but females live 3 to 4 times as long (12 to 15 years).

◆ Tarantula hairs have barbs on them! The spiders shoot the hairs at attackers to irritate their skin, eyes, nose, or mouth.

◆ Some tarantulas in Sri Lanka and India have similar commensal relationships with small frogs.

◆ The collective noun for a group of frogs is an "army."

COMMON EASTERN FIREFLY

FEMME FATALE FIREFLY

PARASITISM

Photinus pyralis
(fo-tin-us pie-ral-lus)

Photuris versicolor
(fo-too-rus ver-see-color)

*F*ireflies, also known as "lightning bugs," flash their luminescent abdomens to attract a mate. Males and females blink their lights in different patterns so they can find each other in the dark. A remarkable interaction between two kinds of chemicals—"luciferases" and "luciferins"—allows them to do this. The common eastern firefly also creates another chemical, a steroid called "lucibufagin," that makes them taste terrible to birds and other predators. But the larger femme fatale firefly cannot produce this enzyme, so to get it, she tricks the male common eastern firefly. She flashes her light as if she were a female common eastern firefly—and then, after luring in a male, the predatory (see page 5) female femme fatale bites and kills him, stealing his protective chemicals for herself and getting a meal in the process.

Conservation Status

LEAST CONCERN/ LEAST CONCERN

Fireflies can be eaten by frogs, birds, and spiders. But other animals aren't the biggest threat to this beloved beetle—their numbers are imperiled by habitat loss, pesticide use, and light pollution.

What They Eat

In their larval stage, both species of firefly are carnivorous, eating creatures like slugs, snails, and mites. As adults, they may eat nectar or pollen, or nothing at all. And of course, the female femme fatale firefly eats the male common eastern firefly.

Where They Live

Femme fatale fireflies, along with the other species in the genus *Photuris*, can be found throughout North America. The common eastern firefly, however, lives only in the United States. Both fireflies inhabit meadows, forests, and urban areas. It can be difficult to see them when they aren't flashing their lights, as they like to hide under leaves, sticks, and bark.

FUN FACTS

◆ The scientific name of the femme fatale firefly, *versicolor*, means "various colors," a reference to their green and yellow glow.

◆ A single male common eastern firefly has enough defensive steroids to protect the femme fatale firefly for her whole life.

◆ Female femme fatale fireflies are larger and stronger than the males of their own species, making them sexually dimorphic.

◆ There are more than 2,000 species of firefly worldwide!

COMMON JACK MACKEREL

TONGUE-BITING LOUSE

PARASITISM

Trachurus declivis
(track-u-rus de-div-us)

Smenispa irregularis
(smen-is-pa ir-eg-you-lar-us)

The relationship between the common jack mackerel and the tongue-biting louse is truly creepy. As the mackerel swims through the sea minding its own business—sometimes in a group, or "school"—the female tongue-biting louse sneaks into the fish's mouth via its gills. There, the louse clamps itself onto the mackerel's tongue with its powerful legs, bites down, and begins to suck blood. Once attached, the female louse will mate and lay eggs, feasting on the fish's blood the entire time. The mackerel isn't able to remove the parasite from its tongue, so it has no choice but to keep swimming around with a louse in its mouth. Fortunately, most mackerel survive and end up outliving the lice.

Conservation Status

LEAST CONCERN/ UNKNOWN

Though common jack mackerel are often caught for food, they still have a healthy population. Unfortunately, they are in danger of losing their main food source, krill, due to rising water temperatures, which negatively impact krill's reproduction rate. There is no information on the conservation status of the tongue-biting louse, but their population is probably under no immediate threat.

What They Eat

The common jack mackerel mainly eats krill and lanternfish (a small bioluminescent deep-sea fish). The tongue-biting louse feeds on the blood and mucus of whatever fish is unlucky enough to host her.

Where They Live

Both the common jack mackerel and the louse inhabit areas off the coast of Australia and New Zealand, as well as the open ocean. They may be found in the waters near Queensland, the Great Australian Bight, Tasmania, and the Kermadec Islands off New Zealand.

FUN FACTS

◆ The tongue-biting louse is related to the pill bug, the little grey bugs that roll up into a ball when you pick them up. And all baby lice are born males; some adult males change into females.

◆ There's another species of louse called *Cymothoa exigua*, the tongue-eating louse. This species eats the fish's entire tongue and then takes the place of the missing organ, more or less.

COMMON RAVEN

GREY WOLF

MUTUALISM

Corvus corax
(cor-vus cor-ax)

Canis lupus
(can-us loo-puss)

*T*he grey wolf and the common raven are true allies and partners in crime. They're almost always seen together in winter, one animal leading the other to food. Believed to be one of the most intelligent birds in the world, the sleek black raven uses special calls to alert the wolves to danger or potential prey. The grey wolf is a smart and social hunter, and it thanks the raven for its assistance by letting the bird share its kills. Their relationship is one of facultative mutualism (see page 5)—and maybe even friendship! Ravens have been known to play with wolf pups and adult wolves, diving down to peck at their tails. The wolves are happy to join in, leaping up or chasing after the birds.

Conservation Status

LEAST CONCERN/ LEAST CONCERN

There are an estimated 300,000 grey wolves and at least 16 million common ravens across the globe, so conservationists consider them both to be of least concern.

What They Eat

Grey wolves are top predators that play a vital role in the ecosystem. Their larger prey includes elk, deer, moose, wild boar, and bison. The raven is an opportunistic scavenger that will eat eggs, other birds, snakes, fish, turtles, insects, and mammals.

Where They Live

The grey wolf used to be the world's most widespread mammal, but it was hunted by humans. Now they only inhabit portions of Asia, Europe, the northern United States, and Canada. The best place to see the grey wolf in the wild is in the northern part of Yellowstone National Park. The common raven can be found living in the open coastal areas, mountains, forests, and cliffs of North and Central America, Northern Europe, central Asia, and northwest Africa.

FUN FACTS

◆ Grey wolves are born with blue eyes; they change to yellow, gold, or brown in adulthood.

◆ The wolf was eradicated from Yellowstone National Park in 1926 because it preyed on herds of animals like elk. After a huge letter-writing campaign in the 1980s, the wolf was reintroduced to the area to help maintain a balanced ecosystem.

◆ The common raven is sometimes known as the "wolf-bird."

COMMON WARTHOG

BANDED MONGOOSE

MUTUALISM

Phacochoerus africanus
(fak-o-kear-us af-ree-can-us)

Mungos mungo
(mun-gos mun-go)

The common warthog, a kind of wild tusked pig that can weigh up to 330 pounds (150 kg), has a friend in the 22-inch-long (55 cm) banded mongoose, a smaller striped mammal that has a taste for insects. When the warthog takes a break from foraging and lies down on the ground, as many as 20 to 50 mongooses will climb on top of it to eat the parasites living on its fur and skin. They'll even stick their snouts into the warthog's ears to remove ticks! It's a beneficial arrangement for both animals: The warthog gets a thorough grooming while the mongooses get a satisfying meal.

Conservation Status

LEAST CONCERN/ LEAST CONCERN

Due to how quickly it reproduces, the common warthog has a widespread population. However, it faces danger from large predators (such as lions, crocodiles, and leopards), as well as hunting, disease, long droughts (although the warthog can go for months without a drink), and habitat loss. The banded mongoose is under no immediate threat.

What They Eat

You might think the warthog uses its large tusks to hunt prey, but these tough-looking creatures mainly eat grass, fruit, bark, and roots. Sometimes they'll even eat their own dung to absorb the nutrients they missed the first time around! The banded mongoose's diet is mostly made up of insects, reptiles, bird eggs, and fruit.

Where They Live

The common warthog and the banded mongoose can be found in Ethiopia, Mozambique, and other countries throughout sub-Saharan Africa. Both animals spend their days in open bushlands, semideserts, and grass or wooded savannas, and their nights tucked away in the safety of their burrows.

FUN FACTS

◆ It's unusual for mutualism to occur between two different mammal species— the relationship between the warthog and the mongoose is actually the first of its kind ever seen in mammals that are not primates!

◆ Warthogs also have a mutualistic relationship with the red-billed and yellow-billed oxpecker. These birds sit on the warthogs' backs, pecking off parasites and signaling if any predators are approaching.

◆ The collective noun for a group of warthogs is a "sounder."

DROOPING SHE-OAK

GLOSSY BLACK COCKATOO

COMMENSALISM

Allocasuarina verticillata
(al-low-cas-er-ree-na ver-tiss-ill-ata)

Calyptorhynchus lathami
(cal-ip-tor-rin-cuss lath-am-ee)

The glossy black cockatoo, the smallest of the five Australian black cockatoos at 17 to 19 inches (45–50 cm) long, has an important relationship with the drooping she-oak tree, a member of the genus *Allocasuarina*. In fact, without these trees, this crested bird with the red-banded tail would struggle to survive. The cockatoo nests in hollows in this species of evergreen, and it feeds almost exclusively on the small seedpods, or cones, that grow on its branches. Like other cockatoos, the glossy black has a very powerful beak, which it uses to rip open the casing around the hard seedpods. Then the empty seedpods and twigs fall onto the ground below, making a gigantic mess!

Conservation Status

LEAST CONCERN/ LEAST CONCERN

The glossy black cockatoo has a stable population. However, these birds face the ongoing threat of habitat loss due to farming, logging, or clearing land for residential housing. Drooping she-oaks are also at risk due to Australia's worsening bushfire season, as they are highly flammable trees.

What They Eat

Although the drooping she-oak's cones make up the majority of the cockatoos' diet, the birds have also been known to feed on other tree species and on insect larvae found within branches and trunks.

Where They Live

Glossy black cockatoos live primarily in and around *Allocasuarina* trees, their main source of food. They can be found in coastal or inland woodlands and tree habitats near waterways. They are native to many parts of Australia, and there is also a small population on Kangaroo Island, near Adelaide. However, recent fires on Kangaroo Island have caused a significant decline in their numbers.

FUN FACTS

◆ Glossy black cockatoos mate for life.

◆ Female glossy black cockatoos have more yellow feathers on their head and broken bands of reddish-orange on their tails, while males have brownish heads and solid orange-red panels in their tail feathers.

◆ A pair of glossy black cockatoos can devour as many as 580 she-oak seedpods a day!

◆ It's especially important to preserve older she-oak trees, as it can take up to 200 years for a natural tree hollow to form.

EASTERN SCREECH-OWL

TEXAS BLIND SNAKE

COMMENSALISM

Megascops asio
(mega-scops a-see-o)

Rena dulcis
(ree-na dull-siss)

While on its nightly hunting rounds, the eastern screech-owl scoops up Texas blind snakes and takes them back to its nest, filled with hungry baby owls. Blind snakes are tiny—only 3 to 12 inches (7–30 cm) long, small enough to be mistaken for worms—and these petite birds of prey could easily eat them, but instead they let them live in the nest, where the snakes perform a valuable service: They devour parasites that might otherwise harm the vulnerable baby owls. In fact, scientists have found that owl chicks that live with blind snakes grow faster and are more likely to survive than owl chicks that don't.

Conservation Status

**LEAST CONCERN/
LEAST CONCERN**

There are more than 500,000 eastern screech-owls in the wild. Habitat destruction threatens their nests, so it is important to take steps to protect them, such as building bird boxes. The Texas blind snake's population is currently stable as well. However, these snakes are targeted by domestic cats, skunks, and birds, and have been impacted by invasive fire ants.

What They Eat

Like most owls, the eastern screech-owl is nocturnal, meaning it is most active at night. Its enormous eyes help it see in the dark, allowing it to catch insects, rodents, lizards, frogs, worms, and even other birds. The Texas blind snake gets plenty of its favorite foods—termites, parasites, and ants—while it is housed in the owl's nest.

Where They Live

The eastern screech-owl and the Texas blind snake are found throughout eastern North America, including parts of Canada, the United States, and Mexico. The owl inhabits diverse woodland environments, and the snake lives among rocks or logs and in open grassy plains.

FUN FACTS

✦ The impressively rapid screech-owl can flap its wings five times per second while flying.

✦ Despite having the word "screech" in its name, the eastern screech-owl has a rather soft call that sounds a little like the muffled whinnying of a horse.

✦ The Texas blind snake is not actually blind. However, it does struggle to see and relies heavily on its sense of smell to hunt.

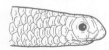

EGYPTIAN SPINY-TAILED LIZARD

ARABIAN FATTAIL SCORPION

MUTUALISM

Uromastyx aegyptia
(you-row-ma-sticks ay-jip-tee-a)

Androctonus crassicauda
(an-drock-toe-nus crass-ee-caw-da)

Both the Egyptian spiny-tailed lizard and the Arabian fattail scorpion have mighty tails, and both use them to fight off predators. The lizard's tail is covered in short, sharp spines; when a threat approaches, this prehistoric-looking reptile protects itself by thrashing its tail about wildly, smacking anything that gets too close. The tiny Arabian fattail scorpion has a many-jointed tail with a stinger on the end. Its venom is extremely toxic, making it one of the most dangerous scorpions in the world. These two tough creatures don't harm each other, though—instead, they help each other out. The lizard lets the scorpion take shelter from the scorching desert heat in its underground burrow, and the scorpion pays the lizard back by warding off predators.

Conservation Status

VULNERABLE/ UNKNOWN

The Egyptian spiny-tailed lizard is struggling to survive, having lost about 30 percent of its population in the past 15 years due to habitat loss, car-related deaths and injuries, and poaching for the pet trade and for medicinal purposes. Little is known about the conservation status of the Arabian fattail scorpion, but scientists believe it is widespread throughout the deserts where it lives.

What They Eat

Despite its intimidating appearance, the Egyptian spiny-tailed lizard is an herbivore, meaning it eats only plants. The fattail scorpion mostly eats insects, rodents, and even other scorpions!

Where They Live

The Egyptian spiny-tailed lizard and the Arabian fattail scorpion can both be found in Egypt, Iran, Jordan, Iraq, Israel, Syria, and the Arabian Peninsula. They prefer to roam on rocky, open ground near their burrows. Daytime temperatures in the desert are incredibly hot, so the lizard and scorpion shelter in their burrows until dusk, when they venture out in search of dinner.

FUN FACTS

◆ Scorpions with thicker tails and thinner pincers are generally more venomous than other kinds, and the Arabian fattail scorpion is no exception!

◆ The fattail scorpion's scientific name, *Androctonus*, means "man killer."

◆ Spiny-tailed lizards can change color! When it's cold, their skin becomes darker to absorb warmth. When it's hot, they turn a creamy yellow color, which helps reflect the sun's heat.

EMPEROR SHRIMP

SPANISH DANCER

COMMENSALISM

Periclimenes imperator
(per–ee–clim–en–ees im–per–a–tor)

Hexabranchus sanguineus
(hecks–a–brank–us san–gwin–ee–us)

In this elegant example of phoresy (see page 5), the emperor shrimp lives atop the Spanish dancer, a type of marine invertebrate known as a "nudibranch," or sea slug. The nudibranch gets its name from its frilly red gills, which resemble the theatrical skirts of Spanish flamenco dancers. From its perch on the back of the nudibranch, the emperor shrimp—which, at a mere 1 inch (2.5 cm) long, is much smaller than its name makes it sound—is not only carried around the ocean floor, but also protected from predators, who know the Spanish dancer is toxic thanks to its vibrant coloring. The shrimp doesn't cause the sea slug any trouble; in fact, some believe their relationship is mutualistic (see page 4), because the shrimp keeps the slug parasite-free.

Conservation Status

UNKNOWN/UNKNOWN

While the details of their conservation status are unknown, we do know the pair face climate-related threats and natural predators. The small shrimp is often caught for the aquarium trade. It is important to keep the Spanish dancer out of the aquarium trade, as its unusual diet makes it very challenging to keep healthy or even alive.

What They Eat

The Spanish dancer eats a range of sponges, some of which are toxic. These toxins are what make the nudibranch itself poisonous to anything that tries to eat it. The emperor shrimp's diet is made up of plant matter and tiny marine animals that get caught in the nudibranch's gills.

Where They Live

Both the emperor shrimp and the Spanish dancer are found in the tropical Pacific and Indian Oceans, around Australia, Japan, Africa, and Hawaii. In the daytime, the Spanish dancer tucks itself under rocks or crevices; it only comes out when the sun goes down.

FUN FACTS

* Nudibranch is pronounced "noo-di-brank."

* Spanish dancers are not the only creatures the emperor shrimp uses for transport. They have been known to hop onto other nudibranchs and sea cucumbers, including the leopard sea cucumber (page 84).

* The emperor shrimp has been spotted eating the Spanish dancer's eggs, which makes the nature of their relationship a little more complicated!

EMU

DESERT QUANDONG

MUTUALISM

Dromaius novaehollandiae
(drom-ay-us no-vay-holl-an-dee-ay)

Santalum acuminatum
(san-ta-lum a-kew-min-a-tum)

*T*he relationship between the desert quandong and the emu is so old and special that it's even mentioned in ancient Aboriginal myths and legends, or "dreaming stories." The desert quandong tree typically grows around 10 feet (3 m) tall and produces small red fruits. These sweet fruits are one of the emu's favorite foods. Although they can't fly, these long-legged birds have no trouble reaching the fruits, as they stand 5 to 6 feet (1.6–1.9 m) tall—they're the second-tallest birds in the world! After the emus have eaten loads of quandong fruits, the seeds pass through their digestive system and are eliminated in the bird's droppings, ready to germinate and grow. In this way, the plant is able to spread to new places. This relationship is an excellent example of facultative mutualism (see page 5).

Conservation Status

LEAST CONCERN/ VULNERABLE

The desert quandong faces many threats, including fires, land clearing, and invasive species like horses, camels, and rabbits. Traditional custodians of the land are working with local councils in Australia to conserve this vital plant. The emu once inhabited Tasmania, until European settlers hunted them to extinction. They now live across most of mainland Australia, where they face natural predators such as wedge-tailed eagles and dingoes; they are also threatened by habitat destruction, hunting, and cars.

What They Eat

The desert quandong is itself a partial parasite and sometimes sucks nutrients from the roots of other plants. The emu adores the sweet fruit of the quandong, but it will also eat other fruits, plants, seeds, insects, and even small animals.

Where They Live

The desert quandong thrives in hot, dry climates with poor soil, which is why it can survive in southern and inland Australia. The emu is found in subtropical, grassland, and savanna habitats across mainland Australia.

FUN FACTS

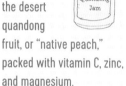

◆ Humans can also eat the desert quandong fruit, or "native peach," packed with vitamin C, zinc, and magnesium.

◆ In 1932, farmers in West Australia asked the government to stop 20,000 emus from destroying their crops. Many emus were killed, but they outwitted the humans to win what's now known as the Great Emu War.

EUCALYPTUS TREE   BELL MINER   PSYLLID

PARASITISM

Eucalyptus spp.
(you-ca-lip-tus)

Manorina melanophrys
(man-or-ee-na
mel-an-o-fi-ris)

Glycaspis spp.
(gly-sass-piss)

*P*syllids are tiny insects that suck sap from the leaves of different eucalypts, or eucalyptus trees. Out of this sap, they make protective coverings for themselves, called "lerps." Small green bell miner birds eat the sugary-sweet lerps—in fact, they love the lerps so much that they fiercely defend the psyllids from other birds and "farm" the insects so they always have a supply of lerps to feast on. There's one problem, though, and it's a big one. When there are too many psyllids living on a eucalyptus tree, that tree is put under immense stress, causing its leaves to die and its health to decline in a process called "canopy dieback." So the more psyllids the bell miners raise, the more the eucalypts suffer.

Conservation Status

VARIED/LEAST CONCERN/VARIED

The bell miner is so aggressive that it doesn't face many threats. And the psyllids also seem to be doing fine. But the eucalypts are struggling. Millions of acres of the Australian forest have been affected by canopy dieback. Species like the grey gum, Sydney blue gum, white gum, and flooded gum are most vulnerable.

What They Eat

Although the bell miner is a type of bird called a "honeyeater," a name that suggests it should eat nectar and fruit, it actually eats only small amounts of each. The bulk of its diet is made up of psyllids and their lerps. Psyllids feed on the sweet sap of different eucalypts.

Where They Live

The bell miner is native to southeastern regions of Australia. This small honeyeater is extremely territorial, chasing away anything that comes too close. They prefer to live in woodlands, bushlands, and open eucalypt forests. Psyllids, also known as "jumping plant lice," live on the leaves of many kinds of plants around the world.

FUN FACTS

◆ Bell miners live in complex social groups of up to 200 birds.

◆ Living in large groups means there are always lots of helping hands—or wings, in the bell miner's case. These birds are "obligate cooperative breeders," which means they require help from other bell miners to raise their babies.

◆ The bell miner uses its loud, repetitive call to scare away other kinds of birds.

FIRE URCHIN

CARRIER CRAB

MUTUALISM

Astropyga radiata
(astro-pie-ga ray-dee-a-ta)

Dorippe frascone
(door-ip fras-cone)

The pink-and-brown carrier crab, only 2 inches (5 cm) long, has a clever way of protecting itself: It uses its back legs to pick up the much larger fire urchin, which can measure 3 to 8 inches (8–20 cm) across, almost four times the size of the crab! It then totes the spiny creature around, using the brightly colored urchin as a shield as it roams along the ocean floor—most predators steer clear of the fire urchin's long, venomous spines. The crab clearly benefits from this arrangement, but what does the fire urchin get out of it? Sea urchins can walk, but they can't swim, and they don't get around very quickly—so getting a free ride from a fast-moving crab gives them access to more food and new feeding grounds.

Conservation Status

UNKNOWN/UNKNOWN

Little is known about the conservation status of either the fire urchin or the carrier crab; however, neither animal is believed to be at immediate risk. Despite its hard outer casing and sharp, toxic spines, the fire urchin still faces some predators. Species like the triggerfish and the wrasse are able to bite through its spines with their strong jaws; then they flip the urchins over and feast on their soft undersides.

What They Eat

Carrier crabs are such messy eaters that the fire urchin doesn't have to look far to find food. It dines on the crab's leftovers, including small invertebrates and algae.

Where They Live

The carrier crab is well camouflaged and is protected by the fire urchin when wandering around at night. However, during the daytime the crab will bury itself in the sand and become almost invisible. To spot one in its hideout, you have to travel to the Red Sea or the Indian Ocean.

FUN FACTS

◆ Due to its vibrant blue spots, the fire urchin is also called the "blue-spotted urchin."

◆ If the urchin loses its spines, it can actually grow them back!

◆ The fire urchin's sting is something like a bee's sting: painful, but unlikely to be fatal to humans.

◆ The sea urchin's anus is located on the top of its body; its mouth is on the underside, to allow it to eat as it travels.

FLOREANA LAVA LIZARD

MARINE IGUANA

MUTUALISM

Microlophus grayii
(my-crow-low-fuss gray-ee-eye)

Amblyrhynchus cristatus
(am-bly-ring-cuss cris-ta-tus)

Both intimidating and magnificent, the prehistoric-looking marine iguana is the only lizard in the world that swims and dives in the ocean, where it finds food. When this enormous reptile is done surfing the waves, it sits very still on scorching black volcanic rocks, absorbing warmth from the sun. The Floreana lava lizard, only 9 inches (23 cm) long, takes this opportunity to clamber up onto the iguana's scaly head and body and scurry around, snacking on parasites, pesky flies, and dead skin. The iguana gets an enthusiastic personal groomer, and the lava lizard gets to dine in the sunshine by the sea!

Conservation Status

NEAR THREATENED/ VULNERABLE

Invasive cats and rats threaten both the Floreana lava lizard and the marine iguana. The iguana is also threatened by pigs and dogs, as well as habitat destruction and tourism. Conservation efforts are needed for both the lava lizard and the marine iguana.

What They Eat

Marine iguanas may look fearsome, but they aren't predators—in fact, they're herbivores, feasting on algae and seaweed that grow on rocks near the ocean, or diving underwater to hunt for algae on the seabed. Along with iguana skin and parasites, the Floreana lava lizard eats plants, fruit, seeds, and insects.

Where They Live

The lava lizard has a very small range and is found on only one of Ecuador's Galapagos Islands— Floreana Island—and the even smaller islands, or "islets," that surround it. The marine iguana inhabits several of the Galapagos Islands, including Floreana, Santa Cruz, Pinta, and Wolf. During the day, the two can be found hanging out together in shrublands, grasslands, on volcanic rock, and even in urban areas.

FUN FACTS

◆ Male lava lizards have been seen doing "push-ups" in front of other males as a way of asserting dominance and marking their territory.

◆ Because of the high salt levels in their food, marine iguanas have evolved a nifty trick of expelling excess salt through their nostrils, like a sneeze!

◆ The collective noun for a group of iguanas is a "slaughter."

◆ Marine iguanas can hold their breath for 10 minutes or more, and dive to depths of 30 feet (9 m)!

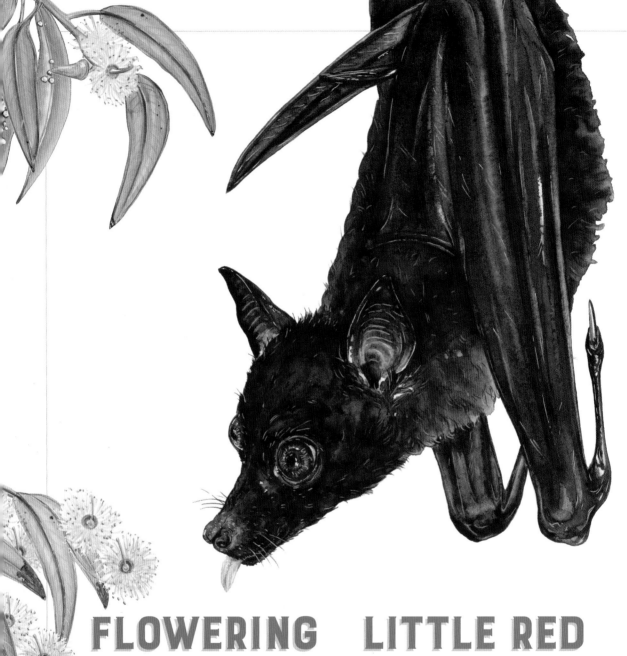

FLOWERING EUCALYPTUS

LITTLE RED FLYING FOX

MUTUALISM

Eucalyptus spp.
(you-ca-lip-tus)

Pteropus scapulatus
(ter-o-pus scap-you-late-us)

When you think of pollinators, a bee probably comes to mind. However, Australia is home to a very important pollinator with claws, wings, and fur: the little red flying fox. This bat's tongue has evolved to be long enough to reach the sweet nectar at the base of eucalyptus tree blossoms. The pollen from these blossoms gets stuck in the flying fox's fur as it eats, and when the bat flies off to the next flower, the pollen spreads and pollination occurs. Flying foxes travel over long distances as they feed, making them fantastic pollinators for eucalyptus trees and indispensable to the ecosystem overall.

Conservation Status

VARIED/ LEAST CONCERN

Unfortunately, the little red flying fox faces a number of significant threats, especially habitat loss due to logging, farming, and urban development. This reduces the number of flowering eucalyptus trees, which are vital to the flying fox's survival. The extreme heat of bushfires has also had a critical impact on the populations of many flying fox species, with thousands dying due to heat exhaustion and stress.

What They Eat

Although technically a fruit bat, the flying fox almost never eats fruit. Instead, it consumes nectar from tree blossoms, and eucalyptus tree blossoms are its favorite.

Where They Live

These bats live and feed on their favorite tree species, the eucalypts, in the northern and eastern regions of Australia. They also live in wet woodlands, mangroves, and bamboo and melaleuca swamp forests. Living in colonies of hundreds of thousands of bats, they flock to eucalypts that are quick flowering, meaning their flowers appear for only a short period of time.

FUN FACTS

◆ The little red flying fox has been known to travel 2.5 to 15 miles (4–24 km) in search of the right food, farther than any other bat species in Australia.

◆ Contrary to the popular belief that all bats are blind, flying foxes have excellent eyesight, especially at night.

◆ Young flying foxes are just two months old when they start to fly.

◆ At just 5 to 8 inches (12–20 cm) long, the little red flying fox is the smallest of the four flying fox species in Australia.

GALAPAGOS DOVE

OPUNTIA CACTUS

MUTUALISM

Zenaida galapagoensis
(zen-a-da gal-ap-a-go-en-sus)

Opuntia ficus-indica
(op-un-tee-a fi-cuss in-dee-ka)

The Galapagos dove often makes its home in old mockingbird nests abandoned in the opuntia cactus, also known as the "prickly pear." It also gets much of its food from the spiny plant. And on Genovesa Island off the coast of Ecuador, there is evidence that a mutualistic partnership has evolved between the bird and the cactus. Bees have disappeared from the island, so the opuntia has come to rely on the dove as its primary pollinator. The bird collects pollen on its wings as it nests or eats and then carries it to other flowers. The opuntia's spines have actually grown softer to allow the bird better access to the plant and its flowers—but only on Genovesa Island!

Conservation Status

NEAR THREATENED/ DATA DEFICIENT

The Galapagos dove is threatened by invasive species such as feral cats and flies. The fly *Philornis downsi* lays its eggs in the dove's nest; the flies then hatch and feed on the chicks. Galapagos National Park in Ecuador is trying to control these predators. The opuntia cactus is widespread, living in many countries around the world.

What They Eat

In the wet season, the Galapagos dove eats caterpillars and cactus flowers. During the rest of the year, it eats seeds that have fallen to the ground. The fleshy pulp of the cactus seems to be the dove's main source of water.

Where They Live

The Galapagos dove, as its name suggests, is native to Ecuador's Galapagos Islands. The birds can be found nesting in the flat pads of opuntia cacti or else on the ground, among bushes, in trees, and in dry or rocky habitats.

FUN FACTS

- Galapagos doves are naturally curious, friendly birds. Hundreds of years ago, they would flock to visting sailors and even perch on their heads and shoulders!

- The fruit and flesh of the opuntia cactus are widely used for medicinal purposes. People also eat their pink fruits and make juice from them—the plant is high in vitamin C and calcium.

- These birds aren't particularly fond of flying, and prefer to stay on the ground or in their nests.

GOLDEN JACKAL

BENGAL TIGER

COMMENSALISM

Canis aureus
(can-us or-ee-us)

Panthera tigris
(pan-there-a tie-grus)

*T*he golden jackal, a relative of the grey wolf (page 40), usually lives in family groups with around four to six members. But if one of the jackals gets into too many fights with the others, it may be kicked out of the group and left to fend for itself. It's difficult to survive all alone in the wild, so solitary jackals have developed a relationship with the Bengal tiger, a large, powerful predator that can reach speeds of 37 miles (60 km) per hour while pursuing its next meal. The lone jackal, called a "kol-bahl," chooses a tiger to follow, then trails it, tracking its moves and eating any leftover kills. Jackals have been known to do the tigers a favor, too, crying out to alert the big cats to nearby prey.

Conservation Status

LEAST CONCERN/ CRITICALLY ENDANGERED

In India, there are laws to protect golden jackals and Bengal tigers from being hunted. However, they still face threats, including habitat loss, illegal poaching, parasites, and disease.

What They Eat

When hunting prey, the golden jackal usually hides itself in the surrounding terrain, waiting for the perfect moment to pounce. In India, it mainly eats fruit, insects, birds, rodents, and other small animals. If a jackal is banished by its pack, though, it relies on the Bengal tiger's leftovers. A tiger's meals include deer, antelope, buffalo, boar, monkeys, and more.

Where They Live

The golden jackal adapts easily to living in a variety of habitats. It has a large range, encompassing central and southeast Europe, the Middle East, north and northeast Africa, Southeast Asia, and India. Bengal tigers live mostly in India, but also in Bangladesh, Bhutan, and Nepal. The commensal relationship between the tiger and the jackal can only develop in areas where the animals' ranges overlap.

FUN FACTS

✦ Bengal tigers have the largest canine teeth of all cats alive today—each tooth is up to 4 inches (10 cm) long!

✦ The jackal is often portrayed as a cunning trickster in North American and European folklore.

✦ The golden jackal has a taste for dung beetles. To find them, it sniffs out animal droppings and flips them over with its paw, revealing the beetles underneath.

GRASS TRIGGER PLANT

REED BEE

MUTUALISM

Stylidium graminifolium
(sty-lid-ee-um grami-nee-fowl-ee-um)

Exoneura robusta
(ex-onner-a row-bus-ta)

When a reed bee lands on the pink or white flowers of the grass trigger plant in search of nectar, a surprising thing happens—the flower smacks the bee! But this doesn't harm the insect or scare it off; it's just a way of making sure the bee will be covered in pollen when it takes off for the next flower. The grass trigger plant gets its name from this unusual mechanism, which works a little like a catapult. When an insect lands on the petals, the pollen-filled male parts of the flower, called "anthers," are activated and swing through the air at high speed, hitting the bee and depositing pollen onto it. And it all happens in only 15 milliseconds! The reed bee clearly doesn't mind, as it's one of the grass trigger plant's most frequent visitors. These two have a facultative mutualistic relationship (see page 5).

Conservation Status

LEAST CONCERN/ UNKNOWN

Both the grass trigger plant and the reed bee are abundant across Australia. However, the pair face potential harm in the form of habitat destruction, pesticides, climate change, and invasive species. As such, it is important to protect them before they are under immediate threat.

What They Eat

Grass trigger plants get their nutrients from the soil. Reed bees feed nectar mixed with flower pollen to their young, and the flowers of the grass trigger plant are their favorite.

Where They Live

The grass trigger plant thrives in almost all bushland environments of mainland Australia and Tasmania, including grassy plains, forests, rocky environments, and around creeks. The reed bee is found across all Australian states and territories. They build their tiny nests in the stems of plants, both native and introduced.

FUN FACTS

◆ Once this plant's trigger has been activated, it can take up to an hour for the flower to restore its energy.

◆ Grass trigger plants are "protocarnivorous," meaning they can catch insects using the hairs on their stems, but they cannot digest them.

◆ Female reed bees block the entrance to their nests with their bottoms, stopping any intruders from coming in.

◆ There are more than 150 species of trigger plant within southwest Western Australia alone.

GRAZING ANIMALS

CATTLE EGRET

COMMENSALISM

Various

Bubulcus ibis
(bub-ul-cuss eye-bus)

The cattle egret shares a close connection with a number of grazing animals, both domestic and wild, and the birds can often be seen near animals such as elephants, zebras, oxen, buffalo, cows, or sheep—even sitting right on top of them! Why do these birds stay so close to their four-legged friends? Grazing animals walk around a lot looking for food, which stirs up small creatures for the egret to feast on. Cattle egrets may also help grazing animals by eating the flies, bugs, or parasites that live on them; however, no one knows for sure if they actually do this, so their relationship is described as "commensal" instead of "mutual."

Conservation Status

NOT APPLICABLE/ LEAST CONCERN

Because of the cattle egret's extremely wide and varied range, its population is not under threat. If anything, its numbers seem to be increasing! However, this bird tends to congregate in large groups of hundreds or even thousands of egrets at a time, so humans often see them as a nuisance or pest, which can cause them to be forced out of their habitats or killed.

What They Eat

Cattle egrets are opportunistic feeders, meaning they're not picky eaters. Much of their diet is made up of grasshoppers, dragonflies, worms, beetles, locusts, spiders, and vegetable matter. They have been known to follow tractors and plows, snatching up insects, frogs, and rodents that flee as the machines plow the fields.

Where They Live

Native to Africa, the cattle egret is now distributed across much of the world, including Asia, Europe, Australia, and the United States. Their habitat is wherever grazing animals live—for example, the cleared pastures where domestic cattle or sheep roam.

FUN FACTS

◆ Cattle egrets are very resourceful when it comes to finding food. They have even been seen hanging around airports, eating insects blown about by the plane's engines!

◆ The egret's bill and legs change color during breeding season, becoming bright red or orange.

◆ The cattle egret is a member of the heron family, though it's somewhat small for a heron, standing only 17 to 22 inches (45–55 cm) tall.

GREEN-BANDED BROODSAC

AMBER SNAIL

PARASITISM

Leucochloridium paradoxum
(loo-ko-klor-idi-um para-dox-um)

Succinea putris
(suck-sin-ee-a pew-triss)

The green-banded broodsac is a kind of parasitic flatworm that survives by being eaten and then living inside other creatures—in this case, snails and birds. The amber snail unknowingly consumes the egg of the broodsac, which grows inside its body, eventually invading the snail's eyestalk and even controlling its behavior! The broodsac needs to be eaten by a bird, so it makes the snail sit on the tops of plants in the daylight, where birds can see it—something a snail would normally never do. Then the broodsac wriggles around like a caterpillar, hoping to get a bird to eat it. Once inside a bird, it matures into a flatworm and lays its eggs, which are dispersed in the bird's droppings. When an unsuspecting amber snail comes along to eat them, the cycle begins all over again.

Conservation Status

UNKNOWN/UNKNOWN

The conservation status of both the green-banded broodsac and the amber snail is unknown. This isn't that unusual for parasites like the broodsac—often people aren't that interested in conserving them. However, it's important to realize that even parasites play a valuable role in their ecosystems.

What They Eat

Amber snails eat vegetation such as grass and leaves, as well as bird poop. The green-banded broodsac has a much more sinister diet. It feeds off its host, absorbing nutrients from the snail until it moves into a bird.

Where They Live

The amber snail can be found in the forests of North America and Europe. The green-banded broodsac needs a moist habitat in order to survive and develop, and the body of the amber snail is the perfect place.

FUN FACTS

◆ If a snail is especially unlucky, it may consume two green-banded broodsac eggs—one for each eye!

◆ When an organism disguises itself as something else to attract prey or be eaten, as the green-banded broodsac does, it is known as "aggressive mimicry."

◆ The collective noun for a group of snails is a "walk."

◆ Snails don't see the way we do: They're able to distinguish between light and dark, but their eyes aren't able to focus or see color.

◆ After the green-banded broodsac has been eaten by a bird, the snail is able to regenerate its eyestalk. Phew!

GREEN SEA TURTLE

YELLOW TANG

MUTUALISM

Chelonia mydas
(chel-own-ee-a my-das)

Zebrasoma flavescens
(zebra-so-ma flav-e-sens)

When the green sea turtle is feeling grimy, it heads to a cleaning station: an underwater area, often near a reef, where cleaner fish will tidy it up. The fish that clean the green sea turtle are called yellow tang. And they have plenty of turtle to clean—an adult green sea turtle can reach a massive 3 to 4 feet (100–120 cm) long and 33 to 441 pounds (15–200 kg)! The bright yellow fish swim in a group alongside the turtle, picking algae and parasites off of its skin and shell. It's a pleasure for the fish, who get to fill their bellies with a nutritious meal. And it makes the turtle happy, too. Removing parasites is good for its health, and a freshly cleaned shell helps it swim more easily.

Conservation Status

ENDANGERED/ LEAST CONCERN

Green sea turtles face many threats: Their nesting habitat is being destroyed, their eggs are harvested and eaten, they're hunted for their meat and shells, they get caught in fishing nets, and they're preyed upon by crocodiles, sharks, and foxes. It's no wonder they're endangered. Fortunately, there are large numbers of yellow tang, but with continuing demand from the aquarium trade, their population could decline.

What They Eat

Green sea turtles have strong jaws and beaks that look like they're made for biting through tough flesh; however, these marine reptiles are herbivores and mostly eat algae and seagrass. The yellow tang needs lots of algae in order to survive, and cleaning the turtle's shell and skin is a perfect way to get it.

Where They Live

Green sea turtles can be found across the Indo-Pacific in both tropical and subtropical climates. The yellow tang's range is limited to the waters surrounding Hawaii, and the fish is only rarely spotted elsewhere.

FUN FACTS

◆ The yellow tang can camouflage itself to stay safe: At night, its bright lemon color fades to a darker yellow-grey.

◆ A yellow tang can live for 40 years. A green sea turtle can live to the ripe old age of 80!

◆ Green sea turtles are the only herbivorous species of sea turtle.

HEATH'S TICK

MOUNTAIN PYGMY POSSUM

COMMENSALISM

Ixodes heathi
(ick-sowds heeth-ee)

Burramys parvus
(burr-ra-mis par-vus)

The Heath's tick makes its home in the fur of the mountain pygmy possum, a small marsupial, only 4 inches (10 cm) long from head to tail, that looks a little like a mouse and has a long coiled tail. Ticks are tiny eight-legged arachnids that are commonly believed to be nothing but bad news, sucking blood and spreading disease—but most tick species actually play a crucial role in their ecosystems. They are a source of food for many creatures, and they help control animal populations in the wild. The Heath's tick doesn't harm the pygmy possum, and is so small that the marsupial doesn't even notice it, which is fortunate as the possum is the only place it lives!

Conservation Status

CO-ENDANGERED/ CRITICALLY ENDANGERED

The pygmy possum has a very small range and is vulnerable to many threats, including habitat loss, climate change, and invasive animals like cats, foxes, and horses. The Heath's tick shares the possum's conservation status. If the pygmy possum were to become extinct, the tick would, too. Climate change is a tremendous threat to this pair, as they rely on cool temperatures and heavy winter snowfall for their survival.

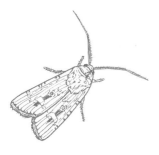

What They Eat

When the mountain pygmy possum isn't hibernating, the nutritious bogong moth makes up a large portion of its diet. During its hibernation period, however, the possum wakes up every now and then to eat fruit and seeds from plants like the mountain plum-pine. The Heath's tick lives off the pygmy possum's blood.

Where They Live

Native to Australia, this pair is found in fewer than 3.8 square miles (10 sq km) of Kosciuszko National Park in New South Wales, and Alpine National Park in Victoria. The area is cold, rocky, and covered in snow almost all year round. At night, the mountain pygmy possum comes out to climb among the large rocks.

FUN FACTS

◆ Australian ticks haven't been studied much since 1970, so the discovery of the Heath's tick in 2018 was especially exciting for researchers.

◆ The mountain pygmy possum is the only marsupial in the world that hibernates! It's also the only one that stores food for later use.

◆ To stay warm while it sleeps, the pygmy possum curls up into a tight ball.

KINKAJOU   BALSA TREE

MUTUALISM

Potos flavus
(po-tos flav-us)

Ochroma pyramidale
(ok-row-ma pee-ra-mid-ale)

The adorable tree-dwelling kinkajou is the only member of the order Carnivora that plays a role as a pollinator! In fact, the balsa tree depends on this nocturnal mammal to help it reproduce. The balsa is a tall tropical tree with pale bark and large, white solitary flowers. The kinkajou loves to drink from these blooms, using its long tongue to lap up their sweet nectar. With its furry golden cheeks covered with pollen, the kinkajou moves from one flower to the next, drinking its fill and pollinating each blossom as it goes. With its eating habits help propagate other trees, too: Kinkajous eat a lot of fruit, spreading the seeds throughout the forest in their dung.

Conservation Status

**LEAST CONCERN/
LEAST CONCERN**

Despite being listed as least concern, the kinkajou still faces natural predators and human-related threats. Their predators include jaguars, foxes, ocelots, and human poachers, who hunt them for their soft fur and meat. The balsa tree is common throughout its range, and is cultivated by humans for its strong, light wood.

What They Eat

You might not expect it from their sharp teeth, but the kinkajou is a frugivore that mainly eats fruits like figs, bananas, and mangoes. About 10 percent of its diet is made up of insects, honey, and the pollen or nectar of balsa trees.

Where They Live

Both the balsa tree and the kinkajou live in the humid rain forest and jungle environments of Central and South America, including Belize, southern Brazil, Ecuador, and Mexico. Kinkajous rarely travel to the jungle floor, preferring to stay concealed in the safety of the trees, where they use their strong hands and tails to get around.

FUN FACTS

◆ Believe it or not, the kinkajou is related to the red panda!

◆ Kinkajous don't rely much on their eyesight. Instead, they have evolved a great sense of smell and touch to stay safe from predators.

◆ Although the kinkajou is the balsa tree's most frequent visitor, it is not the only one. In fact, more than 20 other animals flock to the balsa to drink from its flowers, including birds and bats.

LAYSAN ALBATROSS   OCEAN SUNFISH

MUTUALISM

Phoebastria immutabilis
(fee-bass-tree-a imm-you-ta-bill-us)

Mola mola
(mole-a mole-a)

*M*ost "cleaner" animals live in the same habitat as the creature they're cleaning. But in this unusual pairing, the cleaner is the Laysan albatross, a bird that flies through the air, and the animal it cleans is the ocean sunfish, a giant pancake-shaped fish that lives underwater. So how do these two find each other? During the day, the sunfish swims up to the surface of the water and lies on its side, a behavior known as "basking." The albatross lands on the fish and looks for *Pennella* parasites, which lodge themselves into the fish's flesh. When it finds some, the bird yanks them out and eats them, getting a nourishing snack, and the sunfish swims away free of the harmful parasites.

Conservation Status

NEAR THREATENED/ VULNERABLE

In the 1800s and 1900s, Laysan albatross populations were severely impacted by people collecting their eggs and feathers. They also get caught in fishing drift nets, which killed over 17,500 albatrosses in 1990 alone. The ocean sunfish is listed as vulnerable, and both animals face threats to their habitat in the form of water pollution, climate change, and invasive species.

What They Eat

The Laysan albatross mostly eats squid and octopus, as well as fish, crab, and, of course, parasites. This bird is a surface feeder, landing on the water to scoop up its prey. The ocean sunfish feeds on creatures that move as slowly as it does, including jellyfish, mollusks, zooplankton, crustaceans, and brittle stars.

Where They Live

The Laysan albatross lives on the Hawaiian archipelago in the North Pacific Ocean, and smaller numbers are also found off western Mexico and Japan. After spending months out at sea, the albatross will come to shore to nest in sandy surroundings. The ocean sunfish can be found in warm, open ocean waters worldwide.

FUN FACTS

◆ An adult ocean sunfish can measure 10 feet (3 m) long and weigh more than 4,400 pounds (2,000 kg), but when they first hatch, they're just a few millimeters in size—smaller than a pea!

◆ The Laysan albatross is renowned for its elaborate mating displays, in which the birds dance and click their beaks at one another. Once they've paired off, they'll stay together for life.

LEADBEATER'S POSSUM

GOBLIN FLEA

COMMENSALISM

Gymnobelideus leadbeateri
(jim-no-belly-day-us led-beat-er-eye)

Stephanocircus domrowi
(stef-an-o-circus dom-row-eye)

The Leadbeater's possum, or fairy possum, is a small Australian marsupial, only 12 inches (30 cm) long, that lives in the tops of some of the tallest trees in the world! Its grey coat and long tail are home to the goblin flea, a hairy, six-legged flightless insect. Although the flea is considered an ectoparasite (a parasite that lives on the outside of its host), it does not harm the possum. During its larval stage, the flea eats flakes of skin and other debris off the floor of the possum's nest. Once the larva develops into an adult flea, it climbs onto the possum and lives out its life in the soft fur of this nocturnal creature.

Conservation Status

CRITICALLY ENDANGERED/ CRITICALLY CO-ENDANGERED

Both the possum and the flea are critically endangered because of bushfires, logging, and climate change. In 2009, almost half of the possum's range was destroyed during the Black Saturday fires in Victoria, Australia. Since the goblin flea lives only on the Leadbeater's possum, its future is completely dependent on the marsupial's survival.

What They Eat

The Leadbeater's possum gets nutrients from licking the honeydew, gum, and sap secreted by eucalyptus and acacia trees. Occasionally it will supplement its diet with small insects and spiders. The goblin flea feeds on the possum's dead skin and small amounts of blood.

Where They Live

Found only in a small region of Australia, these two animals inhabit forests around the Central Highlands of Victoria consisting of mountain ash, shining gum, and alpine ash trees. The Leadbeater's possum prefers to live in the hollows of dead trees, which are usually the result of natural bushfires. To help boost the fairy possum's population, 1 million trees were planted across its habitat from 2014 to 2018.

FUN FACTS

❧ After not being seen for around 50 years, the Leadbeater's possum was thought to have gone extinct, until it was rediscovered in 1961.

❧ Baby possums, like all marsupials, are born before they're fully developed. They then live in their mother's pouch for several weeks or months until they're ready to go out on their own.

❧ The Leadbeater's possum and the goblin flea are thought to have spent thousands of years evolving alongside each other.

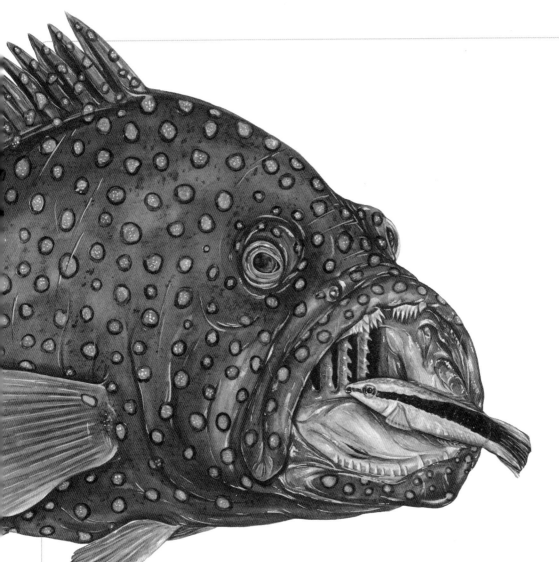

LEOPARD CORAL GROUPER

BLUESTREAK CLEANER WRASSE

MUTUALISM

Plectropomus leopardus
(pleck-tro-po-mus lep-ar-dus)

Labroides dimidiatus
(lab-roy-dees dim-ee-dee-a-tus)

The bluestreak cleaner wrasse, a small fish measuring only 4 inches (10 cm) on average, spends its days pampering the much larger leopard coral grouper, a blue-spotted fish that can grow to be 14 to 47 inches (35–120 cm) long. There's a hint to the nature of their relationship in the wrasse's name—like the yellow tang (page 72), this wrasse is a cleaner fish. The wrasse sets up a cleaning station for the bigger fish to swim into, usually in an empty nook or cranny safe from potential predators. Then the grouper swims up and opens its mouth, allowing the cleaner wrasse to get to work eating parasites, leftover food, debris, and diseased tissue out of its mouth and gills.

Conservation Status

LEAST CONCERN/ LEAST CONCERN

Both the leopard coral grouper and the bluestreak cleaner wrasse are overfished in many areas. Nevertheless, their populations are currently stable in most places. However, the cleaner wrasse is often collected for the aquarium trade, which could threaten its numbers in the future.

What They Eat

Fortunately for the bluestreak cleaner wrasse, the leopard coral grouper isn't interested in eating it. Instead, the grouper feeds on other species of fish and crustaceans. Other than the parasites, scraps, and debris it finds in the grouper's mouth and gills, cleaner wrasse also eat crustaceans.

Where They Live

Found in the tropical waters of the Western Indo-Pacific, this pair can be spotted at depths of 10 to 328 feet (3–100 m) off the coasts of Australia, Thailand, Japan, Fiji, and other countries. They particularly like to live among coral reefs, so it's no surprise that the Great Barrier Reef in Australia is one of their favorite habitats. At night, they hide under sheltered ledges for protection from predators.

FUN FACTS

◆ The leopard coral grouper is able to change to a dull greenish-brown color if it needs a quick disguise to avoid predators (or catch prey!).

◆ The bluestreak cleaner wrasse does a dance by shaking its tail and body, possibly to lure new fish into its cleaning station.

◆ One leopard coral grouper was reported to have lived for 26 years!

◆ Groupers are "protogynous hermaphrodites," meaning they are born female but change into males later in life.

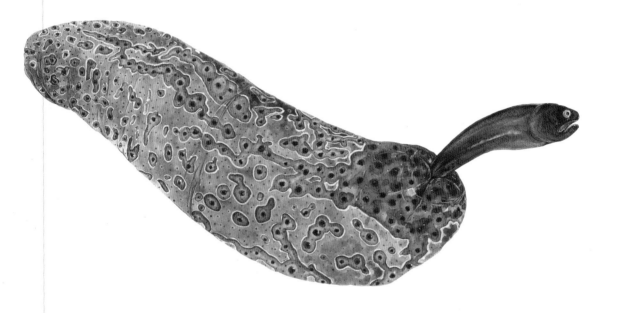

LEOPARD SEA CUCUMBER   PINHEAD PEARLFISH

COMMENSALISM

Bohadschia argus
(bo-had-sha ar-gus)

Encheliophis boraborensis
(en-chel-ee-o-fiss bor-a-bor-en-sus)

*P*inhead pearlfish have found a very unlikely place to call home—inside the anus of the leopard sea cucumber, a long, tubular creature that roams the ocean floor at a snail's pace. Thanks to the size and shape of the pearlfish—they can grow as long as 12 inches (30 cm) and are very thin—they have plenty of room to make themselves comfortable inside the sea cucumber's body cavity, and will either back in or turn around so that they're facing the ocean floor, where they can keep an eye on what's happening outside. And since most predators don't enjoy the taste of sea cucumber, the fish are as safe as can be. Fortunately, the pinhead pearlfish doesn't harm its spotted host.

Conservation Status

LEAST CONCERN/ LEAST CONCERN

Tucked away inside the body of the sea cucumber, the pearlfish faces very few threats. However, the fate of the leopard sea cucumber may not be so bright: They are often caught and sold as food, as many cultures consider them a delicacy both fresh and dried.

What They Eat

At night, the pearlfish leaves the safety of the sea cucumber's body to search for small fish and shrimp to eat. The sea cucumber sucks up sand through its mouth opening, sifts through it for anything edible, absorbs what it can use, and expels the leftover waste.

Where They Live

Found at depths of up to 66 feet (20 m), this pair lives within the Indo-Pacific region, including the waters around Australia, Indonesia, China, and French Polynesia. Different kinds of sea cucumbers live on the ocean floor all around the world, as well as in coral reefs and sometimes in tide pools.

FUN FACTS

◆ A leopard sea cucumber can have five or more pearlfish living inside of it at one time!

◆ Sea cucumbers are related to starfish and sea urchins.

◆ Some species of pearlfish are parasitic and will eat the sea cucumber's internal organs.

◆ The leopard sea cucumber is neither fruit nor vegetable, despite its name—it's a marine invertebrate that usually measures about 14 inches (36 cm) long.

MONARCH BUTTERFLY

VICEROY BUTTERFLY

MUTUALISM

Danaus plexippus
(dan-ay-us plex-ip-pus)

Limenitis archippus
(lim-en-it-us ark-ip-pus)

The regal monarch butterfly has many imitators, perhaps none more successful than the viceroy butterfly, which has evolved to look almost (but not completely!) identical—this mimic is somewhat smaller than the monarch and has an extra black line on its lower wing. But no matter! Predators aren't able to tell the two species apart, which works to both butterflies' advantage—if a bird has learned to avoid one orange-and-black butterfly, it will avoid them all. Both the monarch and the viceroy taste terrible to birds and will upset their stomachs, making this an example of "Müllerian mimicry": when two species, both of whom are toxic or foul-tasting on their own, evolve to look alike.

Conservation Status

LEAST CONCERN/ LEAST CONCERN

Monarch butterfly populations have plummeted by 80 percent in the past 20 years, yet the insects are not listed under any conservation acts. The viceroy butterfly is believed to be plentiful, although no one knows exactly how many there are in the world. Pesticides, climate change, and habitat loss threaten butterflies of all kinds.

What They Eat

As a caterpillar, the monarch butterfly eats the milkweed plant, which is full of toxins that make the insect poisonous. Young viceroy caterpillars eat willow trees, whose high salicylic acid content makes the insects taste bitter. As adults, butterflies drink nectar, though the viceroy also eats dung, carrion, and fungus.

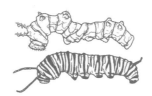

Where They Live

The viceroy butterfly can be found in moist, open areas like the edges of swamps, lakes, and meadows in regions of Canada, the United States, and Mexico. Monarch butterflies are found over a broader range, in North and South America, parts of Europe, and the Caribbean. In areas where the two species overlap, such as the northeastern United States, the viceroy will look almost identical to the monarch.

FUN FACTS

◆ To confuse or distract predators, viceroy caterpillars will hang dung, leaf litter, or balls of silk from the leaves around them.

◆ In areas without many monarchs, the viceroy butterfly has evolved to mimic other butterflies, such as the queen butterfly.

◆ Monarchs breed in Canada and the northern United States, then migrate 2,500 miles (4,000 km) south to spend the winter in Mexico!

MORETON BAY FIG

FIG WASP

MUTUALISM

Ficus macrophylla
(fi-cuss mac-row-fi-la)

Pleistodontes froggatti
(ply-sto-don-tes fro-gat-ee)

*T*he fig wasp and the Moreton Bay fig tree depend on each other completely—theirs is an obligate mutualistic relationship (see page 4). The massive Moreton Bay fig, which can reach 49 to 197 feet (15–60 m) tall, cannot reproduce without the little fig wasp, and without the fig tree's flowers, the wasp can't reproduce either. But a fig's flowers are not like most flowers—instead of blossoming out into the air, they are located inside the plant's fruit-like bulb, called a "syconium." The wasps live and reproduce inside these bulbs. The blind, wingless males never leave, but the females fly off to find another fig to lay eggs in. In the process, they carry pollen from one flower to another, completing the pollination cycle.

Conservation Status

UNKNOWN/UNKNOWN

While the fig wasps are maturing inside the bulbs, parasites are their biggest threat. The fig tree itself is targeted by pests like plant lice or psyllids, caterpillars, and cell-sucking insects known as "thrips." It can also succumb to diseases, such as brown root rot.

What They Eat

Fig wasps live for just a few days, so they don't need to eat! The Moreton Bay fig actually starts its life as a parasite. The "strangler fig" latches onto a host tree and steals its nutrients, growing and twisting around the host until the fig has taken over completely.

Where They Live

Native to Australia, this pair can be found from south Queensland down to eastern New South Wales, as well as on Lord Howe Island. The fig tree has been planted in many countries outside of Australia because of its majestic appearance. The fig wasp has also been introduced to other places, including New Zealand and Hawaii.

FUN FACTS

♦ The Moreton Bay fig can live more than 100 years in the wild, but the wasps live for only 2 to 3 days!

♦ The fruit-like bulbs produced by the Moreton Bay fig are an important food source for a number of animals, including the rose-crowned fruit dove, green catbird, satin bowerbird, and fruit bat.

♦ The Moreton Bay fig tree has buttress roots, meaning that its large, extensive roots sit above the ground.

♦ Fig wasps are tiny: Females are about half the width of a pencil, and males are even smaller— the size of the tip of a crayon!

NORTHERN BETTONG

TRUFFLES

MUTUALISM

Bettongia tropica
(bet-ton-ja trop-ee-ca)

Ectomycorrhizal fungi
(ec-toe-my-cor-rize-al fun-gi)

Truffles, the edible fruits of many types of fungus, are prized by chefs for their rich, earthy flavor—they're extremely expensive ingredients, served in upscale restaurants around the world. They also happen to be the favorite food of a furry marsupial called the northern bettong, or "rat kangaroo." Using its long front claws, the bettong digs deep into the soil in search of the fruiting tubers of ectomycorrhizal fungi, which grow underground on the roots of trees. After feasting on the tasty truffles, the animal scurries off, scattering the fungal spores in its droppings. In this way, the truffle-producing fungus is distributed far and wide. The relationship between the bettong and the truffle is an example of facultative mutualism (see page 5).

Conservation Status

ENDANGERED/UNKNOWN

Unfortunately, the northern bettong is endangered. It has a very small range, is hunted by both native and invasive predators, and is threatened by habitat destruction, drought, and increasingly severe bushfires. While the conservation status of ectomycorrhizal fungi is unknown, this kind of fungus plays a critical role in forest habitats, so it's important to preserve its population.

What They Eat

Northern bettongs forage under the cover of darkness, sniffing out truffles with their powerful noses. Truffles make up about 70 percent of the bettongs' diet. When truffle supplies get low, the little marsupials also eat seeds, roots, underground grass tubers, and insects.

Where They Live

Native to Australia, the northern bettong is only found in northeast Queensland, where it lives in semidry woodlands, rain forests, and eucalypt forests. In Australia, ectomycorrhizal fungi are found in warm climates, growing on the roots of woody plants such as eucalypts.

FUN FACTS

◆ Ectomycorrhizal fungi play a very important role in the ecosystem. They help trees access more nutrients, improving the health of the forest and therefore the ecosystem. This is a symbiotic relationship.

◆ Like its relative the kangaroo, the female northern bettong keeps her joeys in her pouch until they are old enough to follow along behind her.

◆ The northern bettong likes variety in its truffle diet—it eats 135 different species of truffle, many more than most other fungus-eating animals.

◆ Northern bettongs can use their long tails to carry sticks, grass, leaves, and bark to build their nests.

OAK TREE

EASTERN CHIPMUNK

MUTUALISM

Quercus spp.
(kw-er-kuss)

Tamias striatus
(tam-ee-as stry-a-tus)

*T*he eastern chipmunk and the oak tree have a mutually beneficial relationship. The small striped chipmunk loves to eat acorns, the woody nuts that grow from the branches of the towering oak. (Chipmunks are especially fond of acorns from white oak trees.) In fact, a single chipmunk can collect around 165 acorns a day, stashing most of them underground to store for the winter. Once the acorns have been buried, some of them begin to germinate and sprout, and many grow into enormous oak trees. In this way, the eastern chipmunk plays a crucial role in the oak tree's life cycle.

Conservation Status

LEAST CONCERN/ VARIED

Eastern chipmunks are widespread throughout their range, though they face predators such as humans, hawks, raccoons, snakes, wolves, and weasels. The wood of oak trees is often used for flooring, furniture, firewood, wine barrels, and more. But since these trees are so abundant, their population is in no immediate danger.

What They Eat

Chipmunks seem to prefer acorns with small holes in them, as it means there is a bug living inside, which provides an extra boost of protein. In addition to acorns, eastern chipmunks are known to feast on different kinds of nuts, seeds, and fruits. They have also been spotted snacking on mushrooms, bird eggs, frogs, and insects.

Where They Live

Eastern chipmunks are native to the eastern United States and parts of Canada. They can be found as far south as the Gulf of Mexico and have been introduced to Newfoundland. Their ability to coexist with humans means they are often spotted in urban environments. However, their natural homes are forests and brushland. Oak trees share a similar range, growing throughout most of the eastern United States.

FUN FACTS

♦ Chipmunks are the distant cousins of tree squirrels, and both animals are rodents!

♦ Oak trees can live to be 600 years old!

♦ Mature white oak trees can produce 10,000 acorns in a single year.

♦ In winter, chipmunks fall into a sleepy state called "torpor," which is different from hibernation. They slow their heart rate and lower their body temperature, waking up only occasionally to eat.

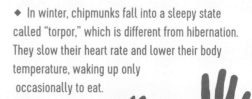

OCEANIC WHITETIP SHARK

PILOT FISH

MUTUALISM

Carcharhinus longimanus
(car-ca-rin-us long-ee-man-us)

Naucrates ductor
(naw-crates duc-tor)

*T*he black-and-white-striped pilot fish, a carnivorous fish that measures about 14 inches (35 cm) long, has found a reliable way to stay safe from predators in the deep and dangerous ocean—it travels with the 11-foot-long (3.5 m) oceanic whitetip shark. But why doesn't the shark eat the fish? It seems that the pilot fish does the shark a big favor. Large sea-dwelling creatures are often plagued by harmful parasites, but since they can't remove the pests themselves, they have to rely on other animals to help them out. Fortunately, the pilot fish is happy to do just that. As it swims beside the shark, the pilot fish munches on parasites as if they were popcorn. It's a win-win situation!

Conservation Status

CRITICALLY ENDANGERED/ LEAST CONCERN

Over the last 60 years or so, nearly 80 percent of the oceanic whitetip shark population has disappeared. The biggest threat to this fish is commercial fishing—sometimes it's intentionally caught for meat or fins, and other times it gets accidentally tangled in fishing nets. While the pilot fish doesn't face the same level of threat, it is still targeted by the fishing industry and taken as bycatch.

What They Eat

Oceanic whitetip sharks will feed on whatever they can, including turtles, tuna, stingrays, and squid. They gather around boats or ships where scraps are discarded. The pilot fish feeds on parasites, small invertebrates, and any leftover scraps from the whitetip's meal.

Where They Live

The oceanic whitetip shark swims in tropical and subtropical waters worldwide. They stay close to the surface of the water at around 115 to 197 feet (35–60 m) deep. Unfortunately, this means they can be captured more easily than shark species that spend their lives at lower depths. The pilot fish, of course, is always with the whitetip.

FUN FACTS

◆ These sharks use "countershading" to camouflage themselves from both above and below. Dark on the top, with lighter bellies, they can blend into the shadows and the sunlit water at the same time.

◆ The collective noun for a group of sharks is a "shiver."

◆ Oceanic whitetip sharks were once the most abundant sharks in open tropical waters.

PAINTED HONEYEATER

GREY MISTLETOE

MUTUALISM

Grantiella picta
(gran-tee-el-a pick-ta)

Amyema quandang
(am-ee-ma kwon-dang)

*T*he painted honeyeater, a small bird with a sharp pink beak, has a close and crucial connection to the grey mistletoe, a semiparasitic plant that grows on casuarina or acacia trees. Mistletoe seeds don't fall to the ground and grow from the soil; instead, they latch onto tree branches and grow from there, their dark red flowers sprouting upward— and the hungry honeyeater is their ticket. These birds devour mistletoe fruits and spread the plant's seeds in their droppings. They have evolved to be completely attuned to the grey mistletoe, even building their nests in and near it. Without the mistletoe, the honeyeater would have a much harder time reproducing— and without the honeyeater, the mistletoe wouldn't find new places to grow!

Conservation Status

VULNERABLE/UNKNOWN

Painted honeyeater habitats are being rapidly destroyed as trees are cut down and land is cleared for cattle grazing. This has caused the honeyeater's population to decline, which affects the population of grey mistletoe. There are estimated to be only about 15,000 painted honeyeaters left in the wild.

What They Eat

The painted honeyeater's diet relies heavily on two species of mistletoe fruit and nectar: the grey mistletoe and the needle-leaf mistletoe. The birds have also been known to supplement their diets with insects and spiders, including the orb-weaving spider. Grey mistletoe absorbs nitrogen from the trees it lives on.

Where They Live

Native to Australia, the painted honeyeater is found all across the continent, except for Tasmania. A majority of the birds live within the Great Dividing Range in Victoria, New South Wales, and southern Queensland. They can be found nesting in yarran trees, which act as hosts for the mistletoe.

FUN FACTS

◆ The painted honeyeater also goes by the name "Georgie," as its call sounds like that name.

◆ Mistletoes are named after the way their seeds are dispersed (through bird droppings, that is). The Old English word for the plant was "mistletan," with "mistle" meaning "dung" and "tan" meaning "twig." That roughly translates to "poop on a stick"!

◆ Painted honeyeater nests are made of sticks, leaves, and other plant materials, all held together by spiderwebs.

PEA CRAB

BLUE MUSSEL

PARASITISM

Pinnotheres pisum
(pin-o-there-ees piss-um)

Mytilus edulis
(my-til-us ed-you-liss)

*T*his miniature crab gets its name from its size—it's no bigger than a pea (0.5–0.7 mm)—which is how it can fit inside the shell of the 4-inch-long (10 cm) blue mussel. But it could have been named the "freeloader crab," as this parasitic crustacean takes a lot from the mollusk but doesn't give much back. It lives inside the mussel's strong shell, which provides fantastic protection from predators and the elements. And it steals food from the mussel, meaning the mollusk might go hungry when there isn't enough to go around. The pea crab's presence may also slow the mussel's growth or distort its shell. When it's not living inside a mussel, the pea crab is a valuable source of food for other marine creatures.

Conservation Status

UNKNOWN/UNKNOWN

The conservation status of the pea crab is unknown. Blue mussels are plentiful. They can be found living together in packed groups known as "beds," and are usually safe from predators and the elements. Some aquatic creatures, such as the black musselcracker fish, have evolved strong jaws and teeth that allow them to bite through the mussels' hard shells.

What They Eat

Blue mussels snag phytoplankton (microscopic marine algae) in their gills, as well as other small creatures or pieces of decaying organic material that float past. The pea crab lives in the mussels' gills—the perfect place to siphon off food.

Where They Live

Blue mussels can be found in the coastal waters of the northern Atlantic Ocean, on rocky shores, or on ocean beds at depths ranging from 16 to 33 feet (5–10 m). Once they reach adulthood, mussels attach themselves to things like rocks and remain there for years. Pea crabs can be found wherever the blue mussels are!

FUN FACTS

◆ Pea crabs live inside a number of mollusks, including oysters, clams, and mussels.

◆ Adult pea crabs like to live alone, which is why you will almost never find more than one fully grown crab in a single mussel.

◆ Mussels can live for up to 20 years.

◆ The female pea crab spends her entire adult life inside a mussel. Male pea crabs only enter a mussel in search of a female whose eggs he can fertilize.

◆ Blue mussels are natural estuary filters, extracting heavy metals, bacteria, and other toxins from the water.

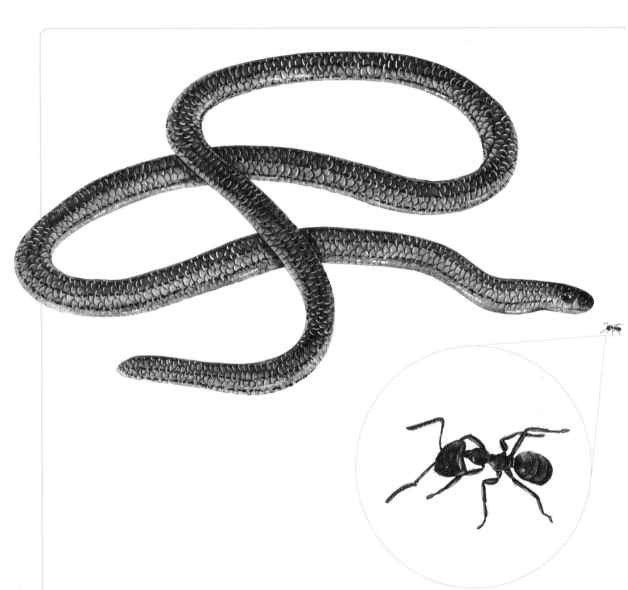

PINK-TAILED WORM-LIZARD   TYRANT ANT

COMMENSALISM OR PARASITISM

Aprasia parapulchella
(a-pray-see-a para-pull-chell-a)

Iridomyrmex rufoniger
(i-rid-o-merr-mex roo-fon-ee-ger)

Only about 8 inches (20 cm) long, the pink-tailed worm-lizard has no legs, so it's often mistaken for a small snake or a large earthworm. It has a complicated relationship with the tyrant ant, a predatory ant that's common throughout Australia. The worm-lizard moves into the ants' burrows, where it hides from predators, shields itself from the harsh sun, and even lays its eggs. It also feeds on the ants' larvae and eggs! Tyrant ants are usually aggressive about protecting their nests, but they don't seem to mind the presence of the worm-lizard and just go about their business as usual. No one knows how the worm-lizard gets past their defenses.

Conservation Status

LEAST CONCERN/ UNKNOWN

Both the range and population of the pink-tailed worm-lizard have increased over the years, so the future of this species looks bright. Even so, it faces threats such as urban development and habitat loss, as well as predation from invasive species such as foxes and cats. The tyrant ant's conservation status is unknown, but it is believed to face the same threat of habitat loss.

Where They Live

Native to Australia, the pink-tailed worm-lizard occupies a few small regions of Victoria, the Australian Capital Territory, and New South Wales, including Canberra, Bendigo, and Queanbeyan, to name a few. To stay hidden from predators, the worm-lizard resides in grassy woodlands, as well as under rocks and in the safety of tyrant ant nests. The tyrant ant can be found all over Australia, except for Tasmania.

What They Eat

Tyrant ants are sugar eaters. They spend their days searching for honeydew and nectar to bring back to their burrows. The pink-tailed worm-lizard survives purely on ant larvae and eggs, largely of the tyrant ant species.

FUN FACTS

◆ Worm-lizards can lick their eyeballs with their tongue, cleaning them of dust, dirt, and debris.

◆ The pink tail of the worm-lizard has evolved to drop off if the lizard needs to escape from a predator. The lizard will grow a replacement soon after.

◆ The pink-tailed worm-lizard also goes by the name "granite worm-lizard."

◆ The collective noun for a group of ants is a "colony."

PITCHER PLANT

MOUNTAIN TREESHREW

MUTUALISM

Nepenthes rajah
(ne-pen-thees rah-ja)

Tupaia montana
(tu-pay-a mon-tan-a)

*T*he pitcher plant and the mountain treeshrew play important parts in providing nourishment for each other. The furry treeshrew pays frequent visits to the pitcher plant to lap up the sweet nectar it secretes from the underside of its lid. While enjoying its meal, the treeshrew poops into the base of the plant, which is shaped like a pitcher or urn and is filled with water and digestive fluid. Poop may not be a good food source for us, but for the pitcher plant, it's perfect—the treeshrew's droppings are full of nitrogen, which the plant needs to survive.

Conservation Status

ENDANGERED/ LEAST CONCERN

The mountain treeshrew has a relatively large population size and range and is not in immediate danger. However, the pitcher plant is listed as endangered. Both are found in Borneo, and they face the same threats as many other plants and animals in the region, such as habitat loss and deforestation.

What They Eat

The treeshrew's diet consists of insects and spiders, fruits, and the nectar of the pitcher plant. The pitcher plant is carnivorous and, aside from treeshrew dung, it consumes a variety of insects that it traps in its mouth, including ants and flies. Sometimes it even eats small animals like lizards and frogs.

Where They Live

The mountain treeshrew and the pitcher plant live in the mountainous regions of Borneo in Southeast Asia, including areas of Sarawak, western Sabah, and northern Kalimantan. This species of treeshrew spends its days hurrying along the ground, rarely climbing up trees or rocks to look around. The pitcher plant is a scrambling vine that usually grows on the ground.

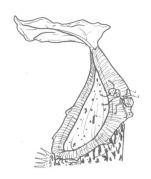

FUN FACTS

◆ The treeshrew may resemble a rodent, but it is actually from the Scandentia order, which is entirely different!

◆ For obvious reasons, this species of pitcher plant is nicknamed the "toilet plant." The largest carnivorous plant in the world, it can hold nearly a gallon of liquid in its "pitcher."

◆ The mountain treeshrew measures about 6 to 12 inches (15–30 cm) long—not including its tail, which adds another 5 to 7 inches (13–19 cm)!

PSEUDO-SCORPION

GIANT HARLEQUIN BEETLE

COMMENSALISM

Cordylochernes scorpioides
(cor-dill-o-ker-nees scor-pee-oi-dees)

Acrocinus longimanus
(ak-row-sin-us long-ee-man-us)

When the pseudoscorpion wants to get around, it boards the back of the giant harlequin beetle, tucks itself under the beetle's exquisitely patterned wing covers, or "elytra," and attaches itself to the beetle's abdomen with silk threads that it spins from its claws. Pseudoscorpions are tiny, no bigger than a raisin (3–10 mm), so plenty of passengers can fit on the 3-inch-long (7.6 cm) beetle, but males have to fight for a space. That's because these little arachnids also use the harlequin beetle as a mobile mating site. The males are extremely territorial, and while female pseudoscorpions can ride for free, only the most dominant male will win a spot. Since the pseudoscorpion uses the harlequin beetle for transportation, their relationship is an example of phoresy (see page 5).

Conservation Status

UNKNOWN/UNKNOWN

The conservation status of this pair is unknown. When it comes to insects, this is not uncommon, as they are small and can be difficult to detect and keep track of. The pseudoscorpion and the beetle are thought to face the typical threats affecting all rain forest denizens, such as habitat destruction.

What They Eat

The harlequin beetle is active during the day and spends its time eating different kinds of tree sap. The pseudoscorpion feasts on termites and their larvae, which move slowly and are therefore an easy target.

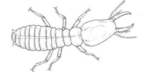

Where They Live

Deep in the rain forests of Mexico and South America, this pair can be found living in rotting, fungus-covered fig trees. When this habitat is no longer suitable for the harlequin beetle, or when it wants to find somewhere to lay its eggs, it will travel to another location, taking the pseudoscorpion along for the ride.

FUN FACTS

◆ The giant harlequin beetle gets its name from its colorful patterns, which resemble the diamond-shaped designs on the costumes of harlequins, or clowns.

◆ Harlequin beetles don't rely entirely on their wings to get around. They also use their long legs to crawl through the trees.

◆ The front legs of the male giant harlequin beetle are often longer than the beetle's body and are used to attract females at mating time.

◆ Although pseudoscorpions don't have a scorpion's recognizable stinger, they do have pincers that can inject venom into their prey.

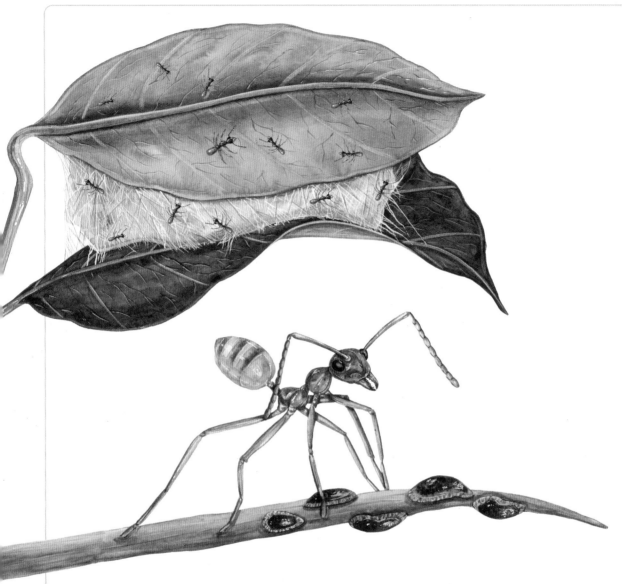

RED WEAVER ANT   SOFT SCALE BUG

COMMENSALISM

Oecophylla smaragdina
(o-so-feel-ee-a smar-ag-dee-na)

Coccidae spp.
(kok-sid-ay)

H umans may have started to farm around 12,000 years ago, but ants have been farming for about 50 million years! However, they don't farm cattle or crops like we do. Instead, they farm soft scale bugs. These little insects, less than a quarter of an inch (5 mm) in size, attach themselves to a plant and suck sap from it, rarely moving once they've found a spot they like. But the ants don't eat the scale bugs themselves—they eat the honeydew, a sugary sweet substance that the scale bugs secrete. The ants are careful not to let too many scale bugs take over a plant and kill it. They also nourish the plants with nitrogen in the form of ant poop, which helps the plants continue to thrive as the scale bugs feed on them.

Conservation Status

UNKNOWN/UNKNOWN

Red weaver ants live in massive groups in a wide range of habitats. As a result, these ants are not thought to be in any immediate danger. Even so, they are preyed upon by tiny parasitic wasps and white crab spiders. Soft scale bug species are seen as pests more often than not, and gardeners and farmers usually try to get rid of them. While they can be destructive, they are also a key food source to many native species.

What They Eat

Red weaver ants primarily eat honeydew, the sticky-sweet residue produced by aphids and soft scale insects that's left on the leaves of the host plant. Soft scale bugs suck the sap of any tree or plant they live on, which can cause the plant to wither, grow poorly, or die.

Where They Live

Red weaver ants live in nests that they build with the help of their young. The ant larvae create thousands of silk strands that the mature ants use to stick leaves together. These ants live in woodland or tropical environments in Southeast Asia, Australia, and the islands of the western Pacific.

FUN FACTS

◆ These ants are feisty and protective and are known to bite those that disturb them or threaten their nests.

◆ Female soft scale bugs don't have wings, but they have been known to float on wind currents to find a plant to live on.

◆ When a weaver ant can't reach across from one leaf or branch to the next, it can form a chain with other worker ants, holding on to one another to bridge the gap. Ant chains can also work together to move large leaves for constructing nests.

10 millimeters

SEA SQUIRT

SPOTTED HANDFISH

COMMENSALISM

Sycozoa murrayi
(sigh-co-zo-a ma-ray-eye)

Brachionichthys hirsutus
(brak-ee-o-nick-thys her-su-tus)

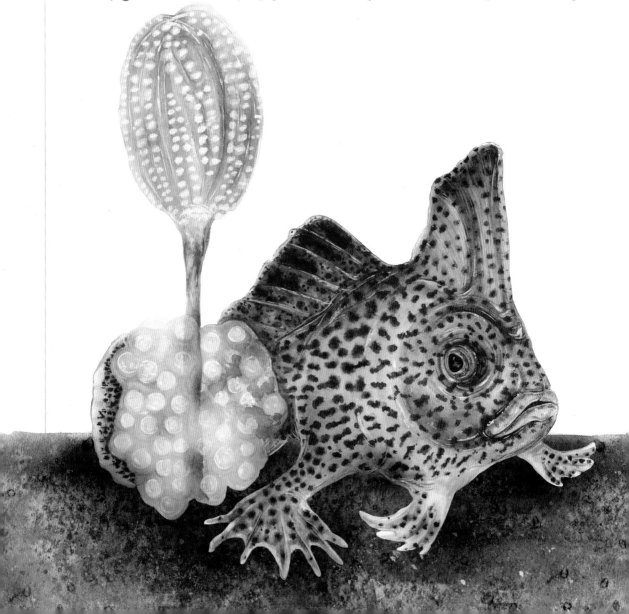

The spotted handfish is a curious creature. Rather than swimming, it walks along the seafloor on its long fins, which are shaped a little like hands! And it will only lay its eggs on a stalked sea squirt, or "ascidian," another unusual creature that doesn't move at all and looks more like a plant than an animal. Every season, the female handfish lays 80 to 250 eggs. The male handfish then guards the eggs for the next 6 to 8 weeks, making sure they don't float away or get eaten by predators. Sea squirts and similar stalked ascidians are vital to the survival of the spotted handfish.

Conservation Status

UNKNOWN/ CRITICALLY ENDANGERED

Both the spotted handfish and the sea squirt have declined in number over the years. They have suffered from habitat loss, being unintentionally caught by the fishing industry, and being hunted by introduced predators (especially the Northern Pacific sea star, which eats sea squirts).

What They Eat

To entice its prey, the handfish has a small lure on its snout, called an "illicium." The illicium wiggles about like a worm and draws in crustaceans and marine worms for the handfish to feast on. The sea squirt is a filter feeder and eats by sifting organisms like nanoplankton through its body.

Where They Live

The spotted handfish lives in only two areas off the coast of Tasmania in Australia. These fish live on the ocean floor and are usually found at depths of 16 to 49 feet (5–15 m). Sea squirts are found throughout the world's oceans, living on anything they can attach themselves to: ships' hulls, rocks, piers, or even other animals, like crabs!

FUN FACTS

◈ Spotted handfish are also known as "prickly skinned handfish."

◈ The spots on each handfish are unique and can be used to identify individuals, just like our fingerprints!

◈ There are more than 2,300 species of sea squirt, and they come in a wide variety of shapes and colors.

◈ Since the sea squirt's numbers are dropping, scientists have placed hundreds of plastic rods into handfish habitats to serve as safe places for them to lay their eggs.

SPONGE DECORATOR CRAB

SEA SPONGE

COMMENSALISM

Hyastenus elatus
(he-as-ten-us el-a-tus)

Porifera spp.
(por-if-er-a)

*T*he sponge decorator crab may be one of the best-dressed crustaceans in the ocean, but its love of dressing up is more about hiding out than standing out! By camouflaging itself in a costume of sea sponges, this little crab is trying to stay safe in the dangerous deep. The decorator crab has unusual hooked hairs on its pear-shaped upper shell, or "carapace"; these hairs act like Velcro, allowing the crab to stick things to itself. The toxic sea sponges it chooses have vibrant red and orange colors, which let predators know that they're not good to eat. Once the crab has attached the sponges to its carapace, they continue to grow and thrive there. Since the sea sponges remain on the crabs for life, this relationship is an example of "inquilinism" (see page 5).

Conservation Status

UNKNOWN/VARIED

Sponge decorator crabs and sea sponges face a variety of threats. These include climate change, habitat destruction, and water pollution. It is important to look after the ocean's precious sponge garden habitats so they do not disappear. Fortunately, these two do not have many predators because the sponges are toxic.

What They Eat

The sponge decorator crab is carnivorous, coming out at night to hunt tiny invertebrates and dine on debris floating around the ocean, as well as leftover animal remains. The sea sponge is a filter feeder, and most of them eat plankton, viruses, bacteria, and debris.

Where They Live

The sponge decorator crab can be found scattered across the Indonesian, Papua New Guinean, and Australian coastlines. It likes to inhabit estuary sponge gardens at around 3.3 feet (1 m) deep, as well as coastal seabeds up to 236 feet (72 m) deep. Sea sponges live throughout the world's oceans, as deep as 3 miles (5 km) underwater.

FUN FACTS

◈ Sea sponges are often mistaken for plants, but are actually very simple marine animals that cannot move around on their own.

◈ These peculiar crabs also go by the name "rhinoceros crab."

◈ There are many species of decorator crab, but all belong to a superfamily of crabs known as Majoidea.

◈ Other kinds of decorator crabs attach anemones, seaweed, or algae to their shells.

◈ The sponge decorator crab releases enticing scents to attract a mate.

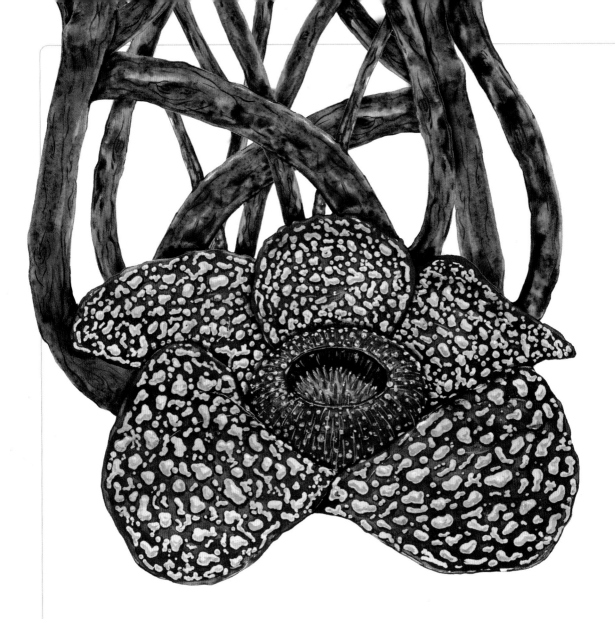

STINKING CORPSE LILY

LIANA VINE

PARASITISM

Rafflesia arnoldii
(ra-flee-sha are-nol-dee-eye)

Tetrastigma spp.
(tet-ra-stig-ma)

eaching a remarkable width of just over 3 feet (1 m) and weighing 22 pounds (10 kg), the *Rafflesia arnoldii*, or stinking corpse lily, is the largest flower in the world. It is also one of the strangest. Instead of having a lovely scent, it smells like rotting meat—an odor that attracts insects like the carrion fly, which then acts as a pollinator—and its five gigantic reddish-brown petals are thick and rubbery. Even weirder, it has no roots, stems, or leaves. That's because it's "holoparasitic," meaning it steals nutrients, water, and carbon from its host plant, the liana, a long, woody vine that drapes and winds around trees in the rain forest. Once a corpse lily seed has found a liana to live in, it feeds off the vine for several years until eventually emerging as a large bud. This flower cannot reproduce—or live at all—without the liana vine.

Conservation Status

UNKNOWN/VARIED

The stinking corpse lily faces habitat destruction and other environmental disturbances from tourism, but it also has another problem: a challenging reproductive process. The plant relies on cross-pollination between male and female flowers, but as there are so few of them left in the wild, many of the massive blooms are never pollinated and, in turn, are unable to reproduce.

What They Eat

Although the stinking corpse lily steals its nourishment from the liana vine, it does not take enough to harm its host. Liana vines have roots that draw nutrients from the soil, and they contain enormous amounts of water.

Where They Live

The stinking corpse lily grows in rain forests, where it thrives in warm, wet weather. It's only found in parts of Southeast Asia, including Malaysia, Thailand, and the Philippines. Scientists don't know how the lily seeds find new vine hosts; one theory is that the seeds are eaten by treeshrews, then pooped out where an elephant may pass and squash the seed into the soil.

FUN FACTS

◆ This large red flower may remind you of a certain Pokémon character named Vileplume. In Indonesia, they call this Pokémon "Rafureissa," in reference to the flower's scientific name, *Rafflesia*.

◆ Don't get this plant confused with the corpse flower, or "titan arum"! That flower is also enormous and emits a terrible odor, but it's an entirely different plant.

SWEET BURSARIA

ELTHAM COPPER BUTTERFLY

NOTONCUS ANT

MUTUALISM

Bursaria spinosa
(ber-sar-ree-a spin-o-sa)

Paralucia pyrodiscus lucida
(para-loo-see-a pie-ro-diss-cuss loo-sid-a)

Notoncus ectatommoides
(no-ton-cuss ek-ta-tom-oi-dees)

*T*his trio has evolved to have a harmonious and cooperative relationship. The Eltham copper butterfly lays its eggs at the base of the sweet bursaria plant. Once the caterpillars have hatched, they make their way to the nest of the Notoncus ant; these ants protect them from predators and escort them back and forth from the safety of the nest to the leaves of the sweet bursaria, where the caterpillars eat their fill of greens. The ants even dig hollows where the caterpillars will complete their transformation from larvae to butterflies. In exchange, the ants consume the sweet honeydew-like substance that the caterpillars produce. This is an example of obligate mutualism (see page 4), as the Eltham copper butterfly relies completely on the Notoncus ant for its survival.

Conservation Status

UNKNOWN/ ENDANGERED/UNKNOWN

Conservation details for the sweet bursaria and the Notoncus ant are not known. However, we do know that the sweet bursaria is eaten by non-native animals like cattle and rabbits. In the 1950s, Eltham copper butterflies had become so rare due to habitat clearing, bushfires, and invasive weeds that they were thought to be extinct, but then they were rediscovered in 1987.

What They Eat

The Notoncus ant feeds on the sugary secretions of the Eltham copper butterfly during its caterpillar stage. The flowers of the sweet bursaria are an important food source for a variety of different insects, including various butterflies, beetles, moths, and bees.

Where They Live

Native to the Australian coastline, the sweet bursaria plant can be found in Queensland, New South Wales, Victoria, South Australia, and Tasmania, growing under the cover of large eucalypts, on rocky hills, or in grasslands. The Notoncus ant is also scattered mostly across the eastern and southern regions of Australia. The Eltham copper butterfly has a much smaller range, restricted to regions of Victoria.

FUN FACTS

◆ The sweet bursaria is also known as the "Christmas bush" because it flowers in December.

◆ The Eltham copper butterfly is thought to live for only a few weeks.

◆ The collective noun for a group of butterflies is a "flutter."

LORD HOWE ISLAND STICK INSECT

TEA TREE

COMMENSALISM

Melaleuca howeana
(mel-a-loo-ka how-e-a-na)

Dryococelus australis
(dry-o-co-sell-us au-stra-lus)

The Lord Howe Island stick insect was believed to be extinct for about 80 years. But in 2001, scientists discovered a group of these wingless stick insects, or "phasmids," clinging to a single *Melaleuca howeana* plant on Ball's Pyramid, a remote and rocky outcrop 14 miles (23 km) away from Lord Howe Island. The stick insect had survived! But it wouldn't have made it without the *Melaleuca howeana*, or tea tree, plant. This dense shrub, which tends to grow on sea cliffs and in other exposed areas, had provided a source of food and shelter for the large six-legged insects, which can measure 5 inches (20 cm) long. Without this plant, the Lord Howe Island stick insect would probably become extinct in the wild.

Conservation Status

UNKNOWN/ CRITICALLY ENDANGERED

This stick insect has been called "the rarest insect in the world." Only 35 have ever been counted in the wild at one time, but scientists hope to reintroduce them to Lord Howe Island through captive breeding programs. Unfortunately, *Melaleuca howeana* faces environmental threats like severe storms, drought, and an invasive vine called the coastal morning glory.

What They Eat

The Lord Howe Island stick insect is thought to feed solely on the melaleuca. It dines under the cover of darkness to avoid being spotted by birds. The insect's dark coloring and large size are difficult to conceal in the daylight.

Where They Live

This stick insect lives in just one region of the 1,800-foot-tall (550 m) Ball's Pyramid, and can be found hiding among the handful of melaleuca shrubs there. Part of an extinct volcano, Ball's Pyramid lies off the east coast of Australia in the Tasman Sea.

FUN FACTS

◈ Young stick insects, called "nymphs," are bright green.

◈ A shipwreck brought rats to Lord Howe Island in 1918, and the rodents decimated the stick insects within just a few decades.

◈ Lord Howe Island stick insects are also known as "tree lobsters" because of their enormous size.

◈ Once a landmark for rock climbers, Ball's Pyramid is now protected as a World Heritage Area, and people can visit only for scientific purposes.

VAMPIRE FINCH

NAZCA BOOBY

PARASITISM

Geospiza difficilis septentrionalis
(geo-spy-za dif-ee-sill-us
sep-ten-tri-o-na-lis)

Sula granti
(soo-la grant-eye)

A strange and somewhat sinister relationship has evolved between the aptly named vampire finch and the Nazca booby. Scientists believe it began like many other mutualistic relationships involving "cleaner" animals that snack on the ticks and fleas found on a larger creature. While cleaning the Nazca booby's skin and feathers of parasites, the finch sometimes extracted a small amount of blood, too. The bird recognized the nutritional benefits of drinking the blood and continued to do so over time. Now, when other food is scarce, these finches depend on the booby's blood, pecking incessantly at the base of the bird's tail and wings until there are open wounds.

Conservation Status

VULNERABLE/ LEAST CONCERN

While the vampire finch's population appears to be stable, its range is restricted and its numbers are small. There has been a noticeable decline in the Nazca booby population over the years. This is thought to be related to diminishing food resources and predators that have been introduced to the islands where the bird is found.

What They Eat

When there is food available, the vampire finch eats nectar, seeds, eggs, insects, and parasites found on the booby's body. During the dry season, when its food supply is disrupted, the finch drinks the Nazca booby's blood. The booby's diet includes anchovies, sardines, squid, and even flying fish.

Where They Live

The vampire finch lives on two small, remote islands, Darwin Island and Wolf Island, both of which are located just northwest of the Galapagos archipelago. These islands are actually the tops of extinct volcanos and are off-limits to tourists. The Nazca booby can also be found on islands off Baja, California.

FUN FACTS

◆ The vampire finch has evolved to have the sharpest beak of all the finch species in the world.

◆ The Nazca booby is one of the few bird species that performs "obligate siblicide." This means that the female booby lays two eggs and if both hatch, the strongest chick (usually the oldest) will kill its sibling after it hatches.

◆ The name "booby" comes from the Spanish word "bobo," which means "foolish" or "clown" and refers to the big-footed birds' awkward and clumsy movements on land.

VERCO'S NUDIBRANCH

BRYOZOAN

PARASITISM

Tambja verconis
(tam-ja ver-co-nus)

Bugula dentata
(bewg-you-la den-tah-ta)

*T*he Verco's nudibranch is a marine gastropod mollusk, just like the Spanish dancer (see page 50). Its vibrant yellow body has electric-blue markings, and it sports elaborate gills on its back that look like tree branches or veins. This species of nudibranch usually lives on top of a particular kind of blue-green bryozoan, the *Bugula dentata*—a creature that could easily be mistaken for a plant, but is actually a very slow-moving aquatic invertebrate. Unfortunately for the bryozoan, the nudibranch is a predator (see page 5) that eats only one thing—the *Bugula dentata* itself! Without this bryozoan, the Verco's nudibranch would lose both its home and its only source of food.

Conservation Status

UNKNOWN/UNKNOWN

It's rare to see these colorful nudibranchs in the wild because of their small size and limited range. Both the nudibranch and the bryozoan are threatened by water pollution, habitat destruction, and climate change. They are also targeted by a variety of predators, including sea cucumbers, fish, crabs, turtles, and sea spiders.

What They Eat

Verco's nudibranchs are carnivorous creatures that prey only on the *Bugula dentata*. The bryozoan feeds on tiny algae particles and phytoplankton via tentacle filters that it extends into the ocean.

Where They Live

These unusual creatures live only in the warm waters off northeast New Zealand and southeast Australia. Populations can be found from Newcastle down the coast to Pambula in New South Wales, around Melbourne in Victoria, near Adelaide in South Australia, and in Tasmania. To find the Verco's nudibranch and the bryozoan, you need to search at depths of 6.5 to 131 feet (2–40 m), in rocky reefs and sponge garden habitats. You will find the pair together almost all the time.

FUN FACTS

◆ There are two hornlike features on the head of the Verco's nudibranch. These are called "rhinophores" and are thought to help the nudibranch find food and a mate.

◆ The eggs of the Verco's nudibranch are just as extraordinary as the colorful adult nudibranchs. They are vibrant yellow and take the form of a ribbon.

◆ Like all gastropods, including garden snails and land slugs, nudibranchs are hermaphrodites, meaning that they have both male and female reproductive organs.

WHITE SUCKERFISH   REEF MANTA RAY

COMMENSALISM OR MUTUALISM

Remora albescens
(re-more-a al-bes-sens)

Mobula alfredi
(mob-you-la al-frey-dee)

*T*he white suckerfish rarely swims on its own; instead, it uses its suction disc to attach itself to the enormous 11.5-foot-wide (3.5 m) reef manta ray, which flaps its gigantic winglike fins as it moves through the ocean. Once it's latched onto the ray's belly, back, or even the inside of its mouth, the suckerfish relies almost entirely on its host for both transportation and food. It feasts on plankton that misses the manta ray's mouth, enjoying a free ride as it eats. The suckerfish may also help the ray out by cleaning parasites and dead skin off its body; if so, their relationship may be one of facultative mutualism rather than phoresy (see page 5).

Conservation Status

LEAST CONCERN/ VULNERABLE

Unfortunately, the reef manta ray is often caught both as bycatch and for its body parts. Its gills are used in Chinese medicine, and its meat, skin, and liver oil are also sought after. The white suckerfish can also be negatively affected by the overfishing of the manta ray.

What They Eat

Reef manta rays are filter feeders and consume large amounts of plankton. The white suckerfish also eats plankton, though some species have been documented eating manta ray poop as well, sifting through the waste to find leftover food and nutrients.

Where They Live

This pair can be found in warm waters in the West Pacific and Indian Oceans. If you scuba dive or snorkel, you may spot these graceful rays, since they often hang out in shallow water near coastal reefs—though they are also capable of diving to great depths! The white suckerfish can be found wherever the reef manta ray is, as well as in the waters of the Western Atlantic and Eastern Central Atlantic Oceans.

FUN FACTS

◆ If there are no reef manta rays around, the white suckerfish will find a shark or a black marlin to act as its host.

◆ The word "manta" means "blanket" in Spanish. These rays do look a little like a flying carpet—or blanket!

◆ A few times a year, up to 150 reef manta rays come together to perform what's known as "cyclone feeding." They whirl around in a circle, stirring up massive amounts of plankton and eating as much as they can.

YUCCA PLANT

YUCCA MOTH

MUTUALISM

Yucca spp.
(yuck-a)

Tegeticula spp.
(tej-ee-tick-you-la)

*T*alk about a long-lived relationship: The yucca plant and the yucca moth have relied on each other for survival for about 40 million years! The spiky plant's soft white flowers provide a safe home for the tiny moth's eggs, and once they've hatched, the moth larvae, or caterpillars, eat the plant's seeds. As for the moth, it is the only pollinator of this tall succulent, meaning the plant wouldn't have a chance at reproducing without its help. They are entirely dependent on each other—an example of obligate mutualism (see page 4). The yucca moths' creamy-white coloration has even evolved to help them blend in with the yucca plants. That is a serious commitment!

Conservation Status

VARIED/VARIED

Yucca moths are a common food source for bats and birds, but their population is currently stable. Climate change poses a serious threat to the yucca plant, however. Many species of yucca plants need cold weather to be able to flower, and if they don't flower, pollination won't happen and their population will decline.

What They Eat

Adult yucca moths live for such a short time that they don't need to eat. As caterpillars, though, they feast on the yucca plants' seeds, which are their only source of food. Since yucca plants are succulents, they have the ability to store water and can survive weeks without rain.

Where They Live

Yucca plants are native to parts of the southwestern United States and Mexico, where they thrive in the high desert. Joshua trees are actually yucca plants, so if you ever visit Joshua Tree National Park in southeastern California, you'll probably spot some yucca moths, too! The yucca moth and the yucca plant are never far apart.

FUN FACTS

◆ Female yucca moths won't lay eggs inside of a flower where another female has already laid eggs. They know that if too many eggs are in one yucca flower, there won't be enough food to go around once the caterpillars have hatched.

◆ Rats also play a role in the yucca plant's life cycle, by eating any leftover seeds and dispersing them in their poop.

◆ Joshua trees can live around 150 years, and the oldest is believed to be 1,000 years old!

◆ The Joshua tree's range is so limited because, around 12,000 years ago, its key means of seed dispersal—the ancient, giant ground sloth, which ate the leaves, fruit, and seeds of these yucca plants—went extinct.

RESOURCES

Many of the animals in this book are endangered; they need our help. Here are leading organizations dedicated to protecting our planet and its precious wildlife. Get involved and help save your favorite dangerous creatures!

World Wildlife Fund
worldwildlife.org

Oceana
oceana.org

Wildlife Conservation Society
wcs.org

The Sierra Club
sierraclub.org

Conservation International
conservation.org

International Fund for Animal Welfare
ifaw.org

Defenders of Wildlife
defenders.org

International Union for Conservation of Nature
iucn.org

International Animal Rescue
internationalanimalrescue.org

The Nature Conservancy
nature.org

ABOUT THE AUTHOR

The author of *A Curious Collection of Peculiar Creatures* and *A Curious Collection of Dangerous Creatures*, SAMI BAYLY completed her degree in natural history illustration at the University of Newcastle. She's drawn to the weird and wonderful—finding the beauty and importance in all living things, regardless of their appearance—and is eager to share her appreciation with others. *A Curious Collection of Wild Companions* is her third book. She lives in New South Wales, Australia.

samibayly.com | @samibayly

The Experiment, LLC | 220 East 23rd Street, Suite 600 | New York, NY 10010-4658
theexperimentpublishing.com

THE EXPERIMENT and its colophon are registered trademarks of The Experiment, LLC. Many of the designations used by manufacturers and sellers to distinguish their products are claimed as trademarks. Where those designations appear in this book and The Experiment was aware of a trademark claim, the designations have been capitalized.

The Experiment's books are available at special discounts when purchased in bulk for premiums and sales promotions as well as for fundraising or educational use. For details, contact us at info@theexperimentpublishing.com.

Library of Congress Cataloging-in-Publication Data available upon request

ISBN 978-1-61519-912-9
Ebook ISBN 978-1-61519-913-6

Cover and book design by Jack Dunnington

Manufactured in China

First printing October 2022
10 9 8 7 6 5 4 3 2 1